P9-BJM-004

# NEW DIRECTIONS FOR YOUTH DEVELOPMENT

*Theory*
*Practice*
*Research*

spring | 2012

# Evidence-Based Bullying Prevention Programs for Children and Youth

**Dagmar Strohmeier**
**Gil G. Noam**

*issue*
*editors*

**Gil G. Noam**
Editor-in-Chief

JOSSEY-BASS™
An Imprint of
WILEY

EVIDENCE-BASED BULLYING PREVENTION PROGRAMS FOR CHILDREN AND YOUTH
*Dagmar Strohmeier, Gil G. Noam* (eds.)
New Directions for Youth Development, No. 133, Spring 2012
*Gil G. Noam*, Editor-in-Chief
This is a peer-reviewed journal.

Microfilm copies of issues and articles are available in 16mm and 35mm, as well as microfiche in 105mm, through University Microfilms Inc., 300 North Zeeb Road, Ann Arbor, MI 48106-1346.

*New Directions for Youth Development* is indexed in Academic Search (EBSCO), Academic Search Premier (EBSCO), Contents Pages in Education (T&F), Current Abstracts (EBSCO), Educational Research Abstracts Online (T&F), EMBASE/Excerpta Medica (Elsevier), ERIC Database (Education Resources Information Center), Index Medicus/ MEDLINE/PubMed (NLM), MEDLINE/PubMed (NLM), SocINDEX (EBSCO), Sociology of Education Abstracts (T&F), and Studies on Women & Gender Abstracts (T&F).

NEW DIRECTIONS FOR YOUTH DEVELOPMENT (ISSN 1533-8916, electronic ISSN 1537-5781) is part of the Jossey-Bass Psychology Series and is published quarterly by Wiley Subscription Services, Inc., A Wiley Company, at Jossey-Bass, One Montgomery Street, Suite 1200, San Francisco, CA 94104-4594. POSTMASTER: Send address changes to New Directions for Youth Development, Jossey-Bass, One Montgomery Street, Suite 1200, San Francisco, CA 94104-4594.

SUBSCRIPTIONS for individuals cost $89.00 for U.S./Canada/Mexico; $113.00 international. For institutions, agencies, and libraries, $281.00 U.S.; $321.00 Canada/Mexico; $355.00 international. Prices subject to change. Refer to the order form that appears at the back of most volumes of this journal.

EDITORIAL CORRESPONDENCE should be sent to the Editor-in-Chief, Dr. Gil G. Noam, McLean Hospital, Harvard Medical School, 115 Mill Street, Belmont, MA 02478.

Cover photograph by Duncan Walker/©iStockphoto

www.josseybass.com

# Contents

Issue Editors' Notes   *1*
*Dagmar Strohmeier, Gil G. Noam*

Executive Summary   *3*

1. Bullying in schools: What is the problem, and how can educators solve it?   7
   *Dagmar Strohmeier, Gil G. Noam*
   This chapter examines how educators can detect bullying, how they can best tackle serious cases of bullying, and how they can best prevent bullying in the long run.

2. The Bernese Program against Victimization in Kindergarten and Elementary School   *15*
   *Françoise D. Alsaker, Stefan Valkanover*
   The basic principle of this program is to enhance teachers' ability to address bullying in kindergarten and elementary school. The program consists of six modules, each corresponding to a specific topic.

3. The Zero program   *29*
   *Erling Roland, Unni Vere Midthassel*
   This program is based on three main principles: a zero vision of bullying, collective commitment among all employees at the school using the program, and continuing work.

4. Making bullying prevention a priority in Finnish schools: The KiVa antibullying program   *41*
   *Christina Salmivalli, Elisa Poskiparta*
   This program is predicated on the idea that a positive change in the behaviors of classmates can reduce the rewards gained by the perpetrators of bullying and consequently their motivation to bully in the first place.

5. School-based prevention of bullying and relational aggression in adolescence: The fairplayer.manual   *55*
   *Herbert Scheithauer, Markus Hess, Anja Schultze-Krumbholz, Heike Dele Bull*
   This is a school-based program to prevent bullying. It uses cognitive-behavioral methods, methods targeting group norms and group dynamics, and discussions on moral dilemmas.

6. ViSC Social Competence Program   *71*
   *Dagmar Strohmeier, Christine Hoffmann, Eva-Maria Schiller,*
   *Elisabeth Stefanek, Christiane Spiel*
   This program defines the prevention of aggression and bullying as a school
   development task. It consists of universal and specific actions that are
   implemented through in-school teacher training and a class project for
   students.

7. Risk and protective factors, longitudinal research, and bullying
   prevention   *85*
   *Maria M. Ttofi, David P. Farrington*
   This chapter presents the results from two systematic/meta-analytic reviews
   of longitudinal studies on the association of school bullying with adverse
   health and criminal outcomes later in life.

8. Resources   *99*
   This chapter provides additional resources on the programs, such as
   webpages and further readings.

Index   *101*

# Issue Editors' Notes

THERE EXISTS AMPLE evidence that a substantial number of children and youth experience, at least temporarily, bullying in school.[1] Bullying is understood to be an interaction between at least two people during which a somehow stronger person (or group) gains power over a weaker person who is not able to defend himself or herself.[2] As the bullying process unfolds over time, the power imbalance increases.[3] Too many young people are chronically involved in bullying as victim, perpetrator, or bystander. Research suggests that bullying roles are moderately stable in preadolescents and adolescents but change a lot in children.[4] Research shows that youth involved in bullying have plenty of intrapersonal, interpersonal, and academic problems.[5] Clearly, stopping bullying in schools is of the highest importance.

Over the past two decades, prevention and intervention programs have been developed by research teams all over the world. Most of these programs have been rigorously evaluated, with strict criteria of evidence used, and many of them are available for schools.[6] Research has also demonstrated that many of these programs are effective.[7] The articles in this volume introduce five examples of evidence-based antibullying programs that were developed in European countries. The program descriptions cover their program goals, main underlying theoretical ideas, program elements, implementation model, and a brief summary of evaluation results.

We hope that educators will find these articles helpful for choosing evidence-based approaches to stop bullying in their schools.

Dagmar Strohmeier
Gil G. Noam
*Issue Editors*

NEW DIRECTIONS FOR YOUTH DEVELOPMENT, NO. 133, SPRING 2012 © GIL G. NOAM
Published online in Wiley Online Library (wileyonlinelibrary.com) • DOI: 10.1002/yd.20001

2    EVIDENCE-BASED BULLYING PREVENTION PROGRAMS

*Notes*

1. Currie, C., Roberts, C., Morgan, A., Smith, R., Settertobulte, W., Samdal, O., & Barnekow, V. (2004). *Young people's health in context.* Geneva, Switzerland: World Health Organization.
2. Olweus, D. (1993). *Bullying at school: What we know and what we can do.* Oxford, UK: Blackwell; Roland, E. (1989). A system oriented strategy against bullying. In E. Roland & E. Munthe (Eds.), *Bullying: An international perspective.* London, UK: David Fulton.
3. Pepler, D. (2006). Bullying interventions: A binocular perspective. *Journal of the Canadian Academy of Child and Adolescent Psychiatry, 15*(1), 16–20.
4. Camodeca, M., Goossens, F. A., Terwogt, M. M., & Schuengel, C. (2002). Bullying and victimization among school-age children: Stability and links to proactive and reactive aggression. *Social Development, 11*, 332–345; Juvonen, J., Nishina, A., & Graham, S. (2000). Peer harassment, psychological adjustment, and school functioning in early adolescence. *Journal of Educational Psychology, 92*, 349–359; Kochenderfer-Ladd, B. (2003). Identification of aggressive and asocial victims and the stability of their peer victimization. *Merrill-Palmer Quarterly, 49*, 401–425; Monks, C. P., Smith, P. K., & Swettenham, J. (2003). Aggressors, victims, and defenders in preschool: Peer, self-, and teacher reports. *Merrill-Palmer Quarterly, 49*, 453–469; Smith, P. K., Talamelli, L., Cowie, H., Naylor, P., & Chauhan, P. (2004). Profiles of non-victims, escaped victims, continuing victims and new victims of school bullying. *British Journal of Educational Psychology, 74*, 565–581.
5. Hawker, D., & Boulton, M. (2000). Twenty years' research on peer victimization and psychosocial maladjustment: A meta-analytic review of cross-sectional studies. *Journal of Child Psychology and Psychiatry and Allied Disciplines, 41*, 441–455; Connolly, J., Nocentini, A., Menesini, E., Pepler, D., Craig, W., & Williams, T. (2010). Adolescent dating aggression in Canada and Italy: A cross national comparison. *International Journal of Behavioral Development, 34*, 98–105; Williams, T., Connolly, J., Pepler, D., Craig, W., & Laporte, L. (2008). Risk models of dating aggression across different adolescent relationships: A developmental psychopathology approach. *Journal of Consulting and Clinical Psychology, 76*, 622–632.
6. Flay, B. R., Biglan, A., Boruch, R. F., Castro, F. G., Gottfredson, D., Kellam, S., . . . Ji, P. (2005). Standards of evidence: Criteria for efficacy, effectiveness, and dissemination. *Prevention Science, 6*, 151–175.
7. Ttofi, M. M., & Farrington, D. P. (2011). Effectiveness of school-based programs to reduce bullying: A systematic and meta-analytic review. *Journal of Experimental Criminology, 7*, 27–56.

DAGMAR STROHMEIER *is a professor at the School of Health/Social Sciences at the University of Applied Sciences Upper Austria, Linz, Austria.*

GIL G. NOAM *is an associate professor at McLean Hospital and Harvard Medical School.*

# Executive Summary

## Chapter One: Bullying in schools: What is the problem, and how can educators solve it?

**Dagmar Strohmeier, Gil G. Noam**

This chapter reviews recent research on bullying from an educator's perspective. It is well known that bullying, a serious issue in schools, can be prevented when educators intervene. But research has shown that it is difficult for educators to detect bullying situations in their school and intervene competently and effectively. This chapter examines how educators can detect bullying, how they can best tackle serious cases of bullying, and how they can best prevent bullying in the long run.

## Chapter Two: The Bernese Program against Victimization in Kindergarten and Elementary School

**Françoise D. Alsaker, Stefan Valkanover**

The Bernese Program against Victimization in Kindergarten and Elementary School was designed to be adaptable to the very different situations and needs encountered by teachers in kindergarten and elementary school. The basic principle of the program is to enhance teachers' ability to address bullying. The program consists of six modules, each corresponding to a specific topic. Teachers are urged to implement the tasks discussed during the meetings in their own classes during the time between the meetings. The program has been evaluated using a prevention-control pre- and posttest design. The informants were teachers as well as children. There was a significant interaction between time (pre- and posttest) and group (prevention and control) as to victimization. Changes in teachers' attitudes toward bullying and their ability to cope with such problems were also significant and in the expected direction.

## Chapter Three: The Zero program

**Erling Roland, Unni Vere Midthassel**

Zero is a schoolwide antibullying program developed by the Centre for Behavioural Research at the University of Stavanger, Norway. It is based on three main principles: a zero vision of bullying, collective commitment among all employees at the school using the program, and continuing work. Based on these principles, the program aims to reduce student bullying by increasing the school's ability to uncover and stop bullying, and eventually to prevent it. The Zero program was launched in 2003, but the work that led to it goes back to the first national steps against bullying in 1983. The program extends over sixteen months as teachers develop their awareness of bullying and their competence in addressing it. Students and parents are involved in the program as well. The role of the school leadership is very important. More than 360 Norwegian schools have carried out the program.

## Chapter Four: Making bullying prevention a priority in Finnish schools: The KiVa antibullying program

**Christina Salmivalli, Elisa Poskiparta**

The KiVa antibullying program has been widely implemented in Finnish comprehensive schools since 2009. The program is predicated on the idea that a positive change in the behaviors of classmates can reduce the rewards gained by the perpetrators of bullying and consequently their motivation to bully in the first place. KiVa involves both universal and bullying specific actions to prevent the emergence of new cases of bullying, stop ongoing bullying, and reduce the negative consequences of victimization. The program has been evaluated in a randomized controlled trial involving 234 Finnish schools and during broad dissemination across Finnish schools (the evaluation involving almost one thousand schools) with positive findings. The program content and the implementation model are presented in this article, and the findings from the evaluation studies are summarized.

## Chapter Five: School-based prevention of bullying and relational aggression in adolescence: The fairplayer. manual

Herbert Scheithauer, Markus Hess, Anja Schultze-Krumbholz, Heike Dele Bull

The fairplayer.manual is a school-based program to prevent bullying. The program consists of fifteen to seventeen consecutive ninety-minute lessons using cognitive-behavioral methods, methods targeting group norms and group dynamics, and discussions on moral dilemmas. Following a two-day training session, teachers, together with skilled fairplayer.teamers, implement fairplayer. manual in the classroom during regular school lessons. This chapter offers a summary of the program's conception and underlying prevention theory and summarizes the results from two evaluation studies. Standardized questionnaires showed a positive impact of the intervention program on several outcome variables.

## Chapter Six: ViSC Social Competence Program

Dagmar Strohmeier, Christine Hoffmann, Eva-Maria Schiller, Elisabeth Stefanek, Christiane Spiel

The ViSC Social Competence Program has been implemented in Austrian schools within the scope of a national strategy plan, Together Against Violence. The program is a primary preventive program designed for grades 5 to 8. The prevention of aggression and bullying is defined as a school development task, and the initial implementation of the program lasts one school year. The program consists of universal and specific actions that are implemented through in-school teacher training and a class project for students. The program was evaluated with a randomized intervention control group design. Data were collected from teachers and students. Results suggest that the program reduces aggression in schools.

## Chapter Seven: Risk and protective factors, longitudinal research, and bullying prevention

Maria M. Ttofi, David P. Farrington

This chapter presents the results from two systematic/meta-analytic reviews of longitudinal studies on the association of school bullying (perpetration and victimization) with adverse health and criminal outcomes later in life. Significant associations between the two predictors and the outcomes are found even after controlling for other major childhood risk factors that are measured before school bullying. The results indicate that effective antibullying programs should be encouraged. They could be viewed as a form of early crime prevention as well as an early form of public health promotion. The findings from a systematic/meta-analytic review on the effectiveness of antibullying programs are also presented. Overall, school-based antibullying programs are effective, leading to an average decrease in bullying of 20 to 23 percent and in victimization of 17 to 20 percent. The chapter emphasizes the lack of prospective longitudinal research in the area of school bullying, which does not allow examination of whether any given factor (individual, family,. or social) is a correlate, a predictor, or a possible cause for bullying. This has important implications for future antibullying initiatives, as well as implications for the refinement of theories of school bullying. It is necessary to extend the framework of the traditional risk-focused approach by incorporating the notion of resiliency and investigating possible protective factors against school bullying and its negative consequences.

NEW DIRECTIONS FOR YOUTH DEVELOPMENT • DOI: 10.1002/yd

*Educators need strategies to detect bullying in their schools and need to be able to apply effective interventions.*

# 1

# Bullying in schools: What is the problem, and how can educators solve it?

*Dagmar Strohmeier, Gil G. Noam*

BULLYING IS A serious problem in schools, and many bullying episodes among students could be stopped as soon as they start if educators intervened. These interventions are, however, rare or ineffective.[1] Teachers are usually not present when bullying occurs and are often never told about the incidents. Researchers found that only 30 to 50 percent of self-reported victims told a teacher about the bullying. But even when teachers directly observe bullying, their actions to stop the incidents are not always successful.[2] Therefore, it is crucial that educators learn (1) how to detect bullying in their schools and programs, (2) how to distinguish light cases from serious ones and how to best intervene differentially with bullies, victims, and bystanders, and (3) how to best prevent bullying in the first place.

This issue of *New Directions for Youth Development* is dedicated to these sets of complicated and urgent topics. All but one state in the United States now have antibullying laws, and many countries around the world show concern and struggle to implement

NEW DIRECTIONS FOR YOUTH DEVELOPMENT, NO. 133, SPRING 2012 © GIL G. NOAM
Published online in Wiley Online Library (wileyonlinelibrary.com) • DOI: 10.1002/yd.20003

policies, regulations, and programs. We are in the middle of a shift from viewing bullying as a painful but typical "kids' thing" to be solved by the peer group to a new understanding of bullying as a serious matter with long-term consequences needing adult intervention. In the process, we need to review what can be done and the evidence that interventions work. Rules and regulations are only one set of needed change; convincing and educating based on evidence is quite another. Thus, the emphasis in this issue is on international research, programs, and even country-wide interventions. At the end we will return to the question of what educators should do when they do not have sufficient funding to implement full antibullying programs, yet want to do more in their schools and programs than improvise or keep the status quo.

## *What is bullying, and how can educators learn to detect it?*

In research and the popular literature, bullying has been defined as a subset of direct or indirect aggressive behavior characterized by intentional harm doing, repetitive aggressive acts, and an imbalance of power.[3] Studies show that educators widely agree with the scientific definition.[4] However, in real-life situations, it is not always easy for educators to identify whether an incident is bullying.[5] Educators are more likely to recognize bullying when the behavior displayed by bullies is direct than when it is indirect.[6] Educators also rate physical and verbal attacks as more serious than social exclusion.[7] Moreover, to infer hostile intent and to distinguish it from playful behavior can be quite difficult for educators in typical settings.[8] Educators often do not pay enough attention to the fact that bullying is usually not a single event; rather, it happens repeatedly over a period of time.[9] Also, when there are clear signs of power imbalance—if a child matches widely held assumptions about victim characteristics (for example, the child is smaller or physically weaker than the others, disliked by peers, or has disabilities) and is perceived as not responsible for the bullying incident—educators are more likely to recognize that bullying is going on.[10] In addition, even educators at the same school may not agree with each other's definitions of bullying or those of their students or the students' parents.[11] In fact, educators usually underestimate the amount of bullying that is taking place. There are also differences between educators and students concerning the perception of the frequency of interventions in bullying: only 25 to 35 percent of students reported that teachers usually intervene in bullying situations; in contrast 75 to 85 percent of teachers reported that they intervene "always" or "often" when observing a bullying episode among their student.[12]

To summarize, research clearly suggests that it is important and necessary that educators better understand what bullying is. More specifically, educators need to learn how bullying can be detected in their settings. Related to the issue of recognition, educators also need to adequately respond in bullying situations.

*How can educators best respond to bullying situations?*
Bullying is often considered to be a relationship problem and a group phenomenon rather than solely an issue of individual perpetrators or victims.[13] This perspective implies that bullying is understood as unfolding in particular social contexts constituted by educators, parents, or peers.[14] When educators, parents, or peers provide social contexts that discourage bullying, much has been done for prevention. And even when bullying has already happened, consistent, immediate, and visible interventions by educators, parents, or peers can stop bullying.[15] Adequate responses by teachers are considered to be most important in a whole-school approach to intervention and prevention.

To explore which strategies trainee teachers use for intervention, Nicolaides, Toda, and Smith found that they were most confident in supporting victimized students and were least confident in their ability to make bullies stop bullying.[16] Thus, the greatest need for training was to learn how to conduct effective conversations with bullying students. Research further revealed that

NEW DIRECTIONS FOR YOUTH DEVELOPMENT • DOI: 10.1002/yd

teachers are more likely to intervene if they perceive the incident
to be serious, if they are highly empathic with the victims, and if
they show high levels of self-efficacy.[17]

These important findings have been incorporated in most
evidence-based prevention programs introduced in this issue that
offer educators strategies for dealing successfully with acute bullying.
In the final chapter of this issue, we will address the topic of whether
change can occur only if a whole school, or even a whole district, bullying prevention program is put in place. Does the evidence support
individual actions, or do such actions always have to be systemic, systematic, and create an overall synthesis of practices?

## How can educators prevent bullying in the long run?

Research shows the best strategy to prevent bullying in the long
run is to apply whole-school evidence-based programs. The most
effective programs engage schools in a school development project
and aim to change the practices in the school and the school culture over time.[18] These programs usually offer both preventative
and interventionist measures. Thus, it is crucial for educators to be
familiar with evidence-based programs in order to make the right
choice for their schools.

*Evidence-based practice* has been defined as an approach that
"helps people make well-informed decisions about policies, programs, and projects by putting the best available evidence from
research at the heart of policy development and implementation."[19] Evidence-based practice has gained importance in recent
years, and standards for research leading to evidence-based practice have been defined.[20] However, there are considerable differences in the implementation of evidence-based interventions and
programs in practice among both countries and various public ser-
vice areas.[21] Especially in the field of education, the adoption of
instructional programs and practices has still been driven more by
ideology than by evidence, in contrast to other sectors of society
such as medicine and agriculture.[22] Consequently, many research

findings that have the potential to support policymakers in the field of education are still being ignored.

Various efforts have been undertaken to define standards of evidence, for instance, by the What Works Clearinghouse (see http://ies.ed.gov/ncee/wwc/), the Best Evidence Encyclopedia (see www.bestevidence.org), the Campbell Collaboration (see www.campbellcollaboration.org), and the U.K.-based Evidence for Policy and Practice Information and Co-ordinating Centre (see www.eppi.ioe.ac.uk). However, the methods used in these efforts vary, leading to inconsistent conclusions regarding which programs and practices have strong evidence of effectiveness.[23]

Anti-bullying programs have been studied more intensely than many other areas of social and emotional interventions in schools. Much credit goes to Dan Olweus and Erling Roland, the Norwegian pioneers of this line of work. Interestingly, many other research-based anti-bullying approaches have also had their origin in Europe, and thus our issue has a strong focus on European work that can help in the next phase of research and application of evidence-based antibullying programming.

This issue of *New Directions for Youth Development* introduces five examples of evidence-based anti-bullying programs. We chose programs that were rigorously evaluated, applying strict criteria of evidence to be represented in this issue. Thus, all programs are based on proven scientific ideas, they have been applied in real life settings several times, and their effects have been demonstrated using state-of-the art analytical and statistical methods. The program descriptions cover (a) the program goals, (b) the main theoretical ideas about the underlying mechanism, (c) the program elements, (d) the implementation model, and (e) a brief summary of evaluation results. Moreover, a systematic/meta-analytic review of longitudinal studies is also covered in this issue. We end by describing common elements found from anti-bullying, program to program, and introduce our four-component model of practices we recommend the education communities implement. We hope that educators will find the approaches helpful to stop bullying in their schools, as well as in their afterschool and summer programs.

## Notes

1. Smith, P. K., & Shu, S. (2000). What good schools can do about bullying: Findings from a survey in English schools after a decade of research and action. *Childhood, 7*, 193–212.
2. Smith & Shu. (2000); Rigby, K., & Bauman, S. (2010). How school personnel tackle cases of bullying: A critical examination. In S. R. Jimerson, S. M. Swearer, & D. L. Espelage (Eds.), *Handbook of bullying in schools: An international perspective* (pp. 455–467). New York, NY: Routledge/Taylor & Francis Group; Fekkes, M., Pijpers, F.I.M., & Verloove-Vanhorick, S. P. (2005). Bullying: Who does what, when and where? Involvement of children, teachers and parents in bullying behavior. *Health Education Research, 20*(1), 81–91.
3. Olweus, D. (1991). Bully/victim problems among schoolchildren: Basic facts and effects of a school based intervention program. In D. J. Pepler & K. H. Rubin (Eds.), *The development and treatment of childhood aggression* (pp. 411–448). Mahwah, NJ: Erlbaum; Roland, E. (1989). A system oriented strategy against bullying. In E. Roland & E. Munthe (Eds.), *Bullying: An international perspective*. London, UK: David Fulton; Smith, P. K., & Sharp, S. (1994). *School bullying: Insights and perspectives.* London, UK: Routledge.
4. Lee, C. (2006). Exploring teachers' definitions of bullying. *Emotional and Behavioural Difficulties, 11*(1), 61–75; Mishna, F., Scarcello, I., Pepler, D., & Wiener, J. (2005). Teachers' understanding of bullying. *Canadian Journal of Education, 28*(4), 718–738; Siann, G., Callaghan, M., Lockkhart, R., & Rawson, L. (1993). Bullying: Teachers' views and school effects. *Educational Studies, 19*(3), 307–321.
5. Hazler, R. J., Miller, D. L., Carney, J. V., & Green, S. (2001). Adult recognition of school bullying situations. *Educational Research, 43*(2), 133–146; Roberts, W.B.J., & Morotti, A. A. (2000). The bully as victim: Understanding bully behaviors to increase the effectiveness of interventions in the bully-victim dyad. *Professional School Counselling, 4*(2), 148–155.
6. Boulton, M. J., & Hawker, D. (1997). Non-physical forms of bullying among pupils: A cause for concern. *Health Education, 97*(2), 61–64; Craig, W., Henderson, K., & Murphy, J. G. (2000). Prospective teachers' attitudes towards bullying and victimization. *School Psychology International, 21*, 5–21.
7. Boulton & Hawker. (1997); Craig et al. (2000); Bauman, S., & Del Rio, A. (2006). Preservice teachers' responses to bullying scenarios: Comparing physical, verbal, and relational bullying. *Journal of Educational Psychology, 98*(1), 219–231; Yoon, J. S., & Kerber, K. (2003). Bullying: Elementary teachers' attitudes and intervention strategies. *Research in Education, 69*, 27–34.
8. Mishna et al. (2005).
9. Mishna et al. (2005); Siann et al. (1993).
10. Mishna et al. (2005).
11. Siann et al. (1993); Naylor, P., Cowie, H., Cossin, F., de Bettencourt, R., & Lemme, F. (2006). Teachers' and pupils' definitions of bullying. *British Journal of Developmental Psychology, 76*, 553–576; Smorti, A., Menesini, E., & Smith, P. K. (2003). Parents' definitions of children's bullying in a five country comparison. *Journal of Cross Cultural Psychology, 34*(4), 417–432.

12.  Pepler, D., Craig, W., Ziegler, S., & Charach, A. (1994). An evaluation of an anti-bullying intervention in Toronto schools. *Canadian Journal of Community Mental Health, 13*(2), 95–110.

13.  Pepler, D. (2006). Bullying interventions: A binocular perspective. *Journal of the Canadian Academy of Child and Adolescent Psychiatry, 15*(1), 16–20; Salmivalli, C., Lagerspetz, K. M., Björkqvist, K., Österman, K., & Kaukiainen, A. (1996). Bullying as a group process: Participant roles and their relations to social status within the group. *Aggressive Behavior, 22*(1), 1–15.

14.  Espelage, D., & Swearer, S. (2004). *Bullying in American schools: A social-ecological perspective on prevention and intervention.* Mahwah, NJ: Erlbaum.

15.  Roland, E., & Vaaland, G. (2006). *ZERO teacher's guide to the Zero Anti-Bullying Programme.* Stavanger: Centre for Behavioural Research, University of Stavanger.

16.  Nicolaides, S., Toda, Y., & Smith, P. K. (2002). Knowledge and attitudes about school bullying in trainee teachers. *British Journal of Educational Psychology, 72*, 105–118.

17.  Yoon, J. S. (2004). Predicting teacher interventions in bullying situations. *Education and Treatment of Children, 27*(1), 37–45.

18.  Olweus, D. (1993). *Bullying at school: What we know and what we can do.* Oxford: Blackwell. Salmivalli, C., Kärnä, A., & Poskiparta, E. (2009). From peer putdowns to peer support: A theoretical model and how it translated into a national anti-bullying program. In S. Jimerson, S. Swearer, & D. Espelage (Eds.), *Handbook of bullying in schools. An international perspective* (pp. 441–454). London: Taylor & Francis; Roland, E., Bru, E., Midthassel, U. V., & Vaaland, G. S. (2009). The Zero programme against bullying: Effects of the programme in the context of the Norwegian manifesto against bullying. *Social Psychology of Education, 13*(1), 41–55.

19.  Nutley, S. M., Walter, I., & Davies, H.T.O. (2007). *Using evidence: How research can inform public services.* Bristol, UK: Policy Press.

20.  Flay, B. R., Biglan, A., Boruch, R. F., Castro, F. G., Gottfredson, D., Kellam, S., . . . Ji, P. (2005). Standards of evidence: Criteria for efficacy, effectiveness, and dissemination. *Prevention Science, 6*, 151–175.

21.  Nutley et al. (2000).

22.  Slavin, R. E. (2008). Perspectives on evidence-based research in education: What works? Issues in synthesizing educational program evaluations. *Educational Researcher, 37*, 5–14; Spiel, C. (2009). Evidence-based practice: A challenge for European developmental psychology. *European Journal of Developmental Psychology, 6*, 11–33.

23.  Slavin. (2008).

DAGMAR STROHMEIER *is a professor at the School of Health/Social Sciences at the University of Applied Sciences Upper Austria, Linz, Austria.*

GIL G. NOAM *is an associate professor at McLean Hospital and Harvard Medical School.*

NEW DIRECTIONS FOR YOUTH DEVELOPMENT • DOI: 10.1002/yd

*Ideally, bullying prevention should start in kindergarten and elementary school. The Bernese program examined in this article trains teachers how to tackle bullying between young children effectively.*

# 2

# The Bernese Program against Victimization in Kindergarten and Elementary School

*Françoise D. Alsaker, Stefan Valkanover*

DESPITE THE GROWING interest in bullying in school, studies that address this issue in kindergarten are still rare.[1] Studies focusing on victimization in kindergarten have clearly demonstrated that the rate at which victimization occurs in the early childhood years is comparable to that in grade school and that it has an immensely stressful effect on young children.[2]

Repeated victimization experiences may elicit intense negative emotions, including feelings of helplessness, worthlessness, and shame. Victimized young children report being afraid of their peers in day care centers and get higher social anxiety scores (teacher ratings) in kindergarten and in elementary school (self-report).[3] Interestingly, the latter result was true for both passive and aggressive victims. As could be expected, school-aged children who are victimized have been shown to be afraid of going to school, which even leads to truancy in older students.[4] Finally, victims' anxiety has been demonstrated to be a consequence of victimization experiences and to make them more vulnerable to subsequent episodes of victimization.[5]

NEW DIRECTIONS FOR YOUTH DEVELOPMENT, NO. 133, SPRING 2012 © WILEY PERIODICALS, INC.
Published online in Wiley Online Library (wileyonlinelibrary.com) • DOI: 10.1002/yd.20004

15

In addition, victimization by peers has been demonstrated to lead to depressed mood in both school-age students and kindergartners.[6] Victimized kindergarten children have also been reported to show increases in depressed mood over a two-year period after entering elementary school.[7]

In sum, all studies conducted on kindergarten children demonstrate that bullying problems occur at this early age. Also, most characteristics of school-age bullying are already present in kindergarten (for example, roles and witness behavior), and they have the same negative consequences.[8] Knowing that victimization may result in stable negative expectations for peer relationships and negative self-evaluations and that negative experiences with peers influence the child's expectations, motivation, and behavior in school, we argue that it is important that victimization prevention begins in preschool and at the latest in kindergarten.[9] In fact, teaching contexts in kindergarten are ideal for implementing prevention programs against victimization. The adult–to-child ratio is usually somewhat higher than in elementary school (depending on the country) and teaching schedules are highly flexible, providing teachers with many opportunities to incorporate program elements in their teaching.[10]

The Bernese Program against Victimization in Kindergarten and Elementary School (Be-Prox) was designed to develop and maintain teachers' ability to handle bullying behavior and prevent victimization. Be-Prox was developed in 1998 in the frame of a research project (and was based on well-known principles used in school programs against bullying and in various programs for developing social–cognitive skills training.[11]

## Main theoretical ideas

There is broad consensus in the literature that bullying is an aggressive behavior systematically targeting specific children and lasting for extended periods of time; moreover, bullying is a social phenomenon involving all children in a class.[12] We also view teachers as involved in the bullying problems themselves because they are part of the class system and often witness bullying episodes without noticing how serious the incidents are.[13] Therefore, teachers have to become aware of their central role in this process. Also, even if an outside expert could help stop an actual bullying problem in a class, bullying problems may come back in the same class or appear in another class some years later. Teachers will regularly confront this problem. Therefore, they are the target group in Be-Prox. The goal is to teach them to detect bullying problems at an early stage, talk about bullying and victimization, prevent occurrences of bullying, and intervene when bullying does occur and stop it.

Be-Prox can be characterized as a systemic and value-oriented approach. It aims to change teachers' attitudes and abilities in confronting bullying and to introduce positive values that are central to healthy interactions in a class.

Teachers' understanding of bullying is often limited, and because many feel insecure and often experience having very little support from colleagues when bullying problems occur, Be-Prox is based on transfer of knowledge and support.[14] Knowledge is important, but it does not suffice. Teachers' insecurity about their right to intervene and their ability to solve bullying problems often prevents them from taking action. Therefore, developing teachers' awareness and offering them support play a central role in the program. Because teachers often need support from colleagues to be efficient in handling bullying, group sessions are an integral part of Be-Prox. We recommend forming groups with teachers from the same school to ensure that teachers help one another solve problems that arise after the course and supervision are over.

All elements of Be-Prox are based on empirical knowledge about bullying:

• Bullying is a social phenomenon; all children and adults are involved.
• It may be difficult to recognize bullying, especially when the forms used are subtle.

NEW DIRECTIONS FOR YOUTH DEVELOPMENT • DOI: 10.1002/yd

- Nobody talks about it, and it is often trivialized.
- Children who are victimized cannot defend themselves adequately and have little support.
- Bullying is highly rewarding for the bullies.
- Bullies are clearly lacking empathy and moral motivation.
- Bullying has tremendous psychological consequences.

## Program elements and the implementation model

In our program, teachers have focused supervision for approximately four months as the program is implemented. We usually organize six group sessions (we used eight in our first implementation of the program) and give teachers specific tasks to work on between meetings.[15] All meetings follow the same basic agenda:

1. Information about specific topics is given.
2. Implications of the new information are discussed.
3. Specific implementation tasks are introduced.
4. Teachers work in groups to develop ways to implement antibullying practices in their classes.
5. Teachers are urged to implement the specific preventive elements in the time between the meetings, and possible upcoming problems are addressed.

The next meeting starts with a discussion of teachers' experiences with implementing the tasks established in the previous meeting.

Since our first implementation of the program, the agenda for the meetings has been changed slightly to meet teachers' needs. For example, we give teachers some more time at the beginning, to learn about bullying and to consider the usefulness of prevention, before they start talking about victimization with the children, and we combine some other topics in a meeting. We now use the term *module* instead of *meeting*, because it makes the program more flexible: one module, for example, can be addressed over two meetings. The overall model of Be-Prox has remained the same since its start, however.

*Module 1: Sensitization: "Subjective attitudes"*

The main purpose of the first module (and meeting) is sensitization. Specific aspects of victimization are presented. Teachers are
encouraged to think about their own attitudes toward children
involved in bullying and to make a commitment to values against
it. Early diagnosis of victimization patterns is emphasized, along
with information about different types of conflicts or aggressive
encounters and bully-victim problems. Because we think that bullying prevention is very much a matter of values, we give teachers
some more time to prepare for the prevention program than we
did at the beginning of our work with Be-Prox before assigning
specific tasks. However, we do start addressing the importance of
communication with parents and ask teachers to begin preparing a
meeting with parents in which they will inform them about their
work to address bullying. In fact, the issue of work with parents is
addressed in all modules.

*Module 2: Bullying may be hard to detect: "Look at it"*

Issues that may interact with the early recognition of bullying and
victimization are discussed, and new information is introduced.
The task given to the teachers in the weeks between the first and
second meeting is called "look at it." We emphasize the potential
of teachers' own "bad feelings" and intuition in the early detection
process. They are invited to observe their students' behavior systematically during the weeks following the meeting. Different
approaches are discussed, but teachers are free to choose a method
they feel comfortable with. They may also fill out questionnaires
that we use in our research. They can decide how they want to
document their observations or how they want to use the information in the questionnaires for themselves.

*Module 3: The rule of silence: "Let's talk together about
bullying and victimization"*

This meeting starts with a discussion of the experiences teachers
have had with their systematic observations. Then the discussion

moves on to information concerning the rule of silence in bullying. This refers to findings that bullies, victims, and the other children never talk about bullying and that adults usually follow the same rule and do not address it either. We focus on how bullies use this rule of silence to gain even more power over the class and the teacher. Then we argue that breaking the rule of silence is a central element in preventing bullying.

Next, we ask teachers to discuss how to introduce the topic in their class. Their task is to sensitize the children, just as they themselves were sensitized to the urgency of preventing (or stopping) bullying. Our experience is that many teachers feel uncomfortable about talking about victimization with the children, specifically when they have not directly observed harsh bullying in their classes. Therefore, we discuss softer ways to address it, starting with the issue of good and bad feelings. Our experience is that children nearly always report bullying experiences when they start explaining what bad feelings are.[16]

### Module 4: Rules against bullying: "The contract"

Bullying is highly dependent on reward structures in the class. The importance of rules, limits, and structure for children's development is discussed. Also, the role of the so-called noninvolved children in (indirectly) rewarding bullies is addressed. Bullying can be prevented or stopped only if new attitudes and norms can be established against victimization of peers. Knowledge about the role of bullying attitudes, bullies' deficits in empathy and moral motivation, and their use of moral disengagement strategies are discussed, as well as the implication of these findings.[17]

Following a description of experiences of various programs, the meeting emphasizes the importance of a positive team spirit in the class and the value of developing a behavior code with the children.[18] Teachers are invited to have a closer look at the Kandersteg Declaration against Bullying that was initiated by the first author in 2007 (www.kanderstegdeclaration.com) and consider using it in their work with the children's parents, their colleagues, and older students. Teachers and their students are free to agree on their own way to define behavior rules and make a contract with another. In kindergarten and first grade, children make drawings describing which kind of behavior should be enhanced or reduced. Because teachers often establish rules themselves without discussing them with the children, the importance of the participation of the children is underlined in order to ensure the commitment of all students.

Feedback on discussions with the children and the implementation of rules has been highly positive. Children are usually eager to work on the rules and produce many suggestions and drawings. Many teachers report that the children were proud of the behavior code they produced.[19]

### Module 5: Take action: "The use of positive and negative sanctions"

Agreeing about a behavior code and even signing a contract is not enough to prevent (or stop) bullying if teachers do not follow up. The topic of this module is the importance of consistent teacher behavior, positive and negative sanctions, and the use of basic learning principles. Previous experiences showed how important it is to discuss these issues in depth.[20] Teachers' insecurity about bullying and also about their role as teachers often inhibits consistent reactions to bullying behavior. We call the task given to the teachers "Take Action," which means that they should systematically and consistently use positive and negative sanctions, remind children about the contract when needed, and reinforce positive behavior.

Teachers are encouraged to talk with the children about appropriate reactions in case a student breaks the rules and about positive and negative sanctions. The role of teachers is central: they must show that they are serious about not allowing any bullying in their class. We encourage discussions about rewarding positive changes in the class and motivating all children to help each other act in accordance with the contract.

Our experience is that the issue of reporting on bullying behavior or requesting help from the teacher versus tattling on peers has to be addressed because tattling is a sensitive issue. Many teachers were concerned about introducing a tattling culture in their classes if children were encouraged to report on rule transgressions regarding bullying behavior.[21]

Teachers' tendencies to excuse aggressive behavior because of possible inner conflicts were intensely discussed in our first implementation of Be-Prox. In addition, the role of the teacher as a socialization agent and many teachers' reluctance to use negative sanctions is a recurrent and important topic. The tasks for the following implementation period are to:

• Discuss fairness, sanctions, and rewards with the children
• Note transgressions against the behavior code
• Reflect on existing reinforcement patterns around victims and bullies in the class
• Look for resources in the class

*Module 6: Developing social competence*

Social competence, empathy, and positive activities are the focus of the sixth, and last, module, and given the theoretical frame of the program, civil courage is emphasized. Teachers are invited to help children take the perspective of victimized children, tell bullies to stop, and report bullying behavior to an adult when they cannot help themselves (see also module 5)—and in general, to engage in helping and supporting each other in difficult situations. We also invite teachers to include physical activities and body awareness as part of the planned positive activities. They are asked to train children in differentiating between aggression and strength. Because victims generally perceive themselves as weaker than others and also are perceived as such by their peers even if physical tests do not support these views, educators need to develop victims' awareness of their own physical competence and strength and provide all children with a realistic perception of the strength of bullies.[22]

Also, because victims have repeatedly been found to have some difficulty in setting limits, teachers are asked to emphasize each child's right to say no and everyone's duty to respect others' limits.

We recommend the use of very clear signs or symbols to communicate one's own limits. Teachers are asked to find adequate teaching material and use it with the children.

### Concluding meeting: Consolidation through prevention goals

We arrange some time, mostly as part of the last meeting, to discuss with teachers how they can ensure that the prevention work will go on after the course ends. We encourage them to define some simple and easy-to-reach goals toward the overall goal of no tolerance for bullying.

By the end of the course, all teachers should have organized a meeting with parents. The issue is introduced as part of module 1, and it is followed up during the course. We offer some support in the form of discussions and provide materials if needed, but we do not participate in the meetings ourselves since we want teachers to experience their own ability to address bullying.

---

## Evaluation results

This program was evaluated as part of a research project. A pre- and posttest design with a control and a prevention group was used.[23] The most interesting sources of information with respect to changes in occurrences of bullying and victimization were the children themselves.

Teacher data yielded no changes in reported bullying behavior for either the prevention group or the control group. Results on being victimized, however, showed significant interaction effects for three of four types of victimization. All changes in the control group were negative: different types of victimization had increased significantly. In the prevention group, scores on physical and indirect victimization had dropped significantly. Verbal victimization yielded no significant results.[24]

Teachers in the prevention group invested much time in the program. Therefore, one could expect them to be eager to show at posttest that bullying problems had declined. Teachers in the control group also spent much time completing questionnaires and organizing our interview visits. Consequently, they could also have been motivated to show that they managed well even without our program. Furthermore, teachers in the prevention group were highly sensitized to victimization, especially to subtle aggressive behavior. Thus, we could also have reported much more victimization at posttest than at pretest just because they were more aware of problems. In sum, there are good reasons to consider the results as valid.

One of the strengths of our project was the multi-informant design, opening up the possibility of analyzing information from the children themselves as observers of bullying (using a peer nomination method). Nominations by peers as "being a victim" were used to create a dichotomous variable (0 = no or one nomination received, 1 = at least two nominations) as an indication of risk of victimization. In the prevention group, there was a decrease of 15 percent in the number of children identified as possible victims. In the control group, there was an increase of 55 percent. We interpreted the increase reported by the children in the control group as a normal pattern when nothing is done to prevent or stop bullying. Other analyses of the peer nomination data gave similar results.[25] This finding corresponds to the results obtained on the basis of teachers' data, suggesting either a decline in victimization in the prevention group or an increase in the control group.

The pretest/posttest comparisons of teachers' attitudes and self-reported behavior also clearly demonstrated that teachers in the prevention group felt more secure in their ability to address bullying. They also reported at posttest that the children helped one another more than at pretest, and they found that children could learn to handle bullying situations. Also, in the prevention group, teachers were significantly less convinced that victimization occurs only "behind their back," or that "some children are born to be victims." All in all, their reports reflected a change toward a new attitude: "Victimization is a phenomenon teachers can be aware of and stop."[26] There were no such changes in the control group.

Another encouraging finding was that teachers in the prevention group developed positive attitudes toward working with the parents of the kindergartners during the project time. They agreed almost unanimously that it was very important to work with the parents and that it made sense to talk with parents about this problem. During this same period of time, teachers from the control group had become rather negative toward parents.[27]

The significant decrease in victimization in the prevention group may seem modest at first glance. However, when compared with the large increase in the control group, the reduction of victimization in the prevention groups must be qualified as substantial. Furthermore, the similarity of the findings based on teachers' reports and children's peer nominations indicates high reliability of the findings.

Farrington and Ttofi included our evaluation results in one of their meta-analyses on school-based programs to reduce bullying and victimization. They used the prevalence data based on peer nominations. Be-Prox was one of the nineteen programs (out of forty-four retained for analysis) that appeared to be effective in reducing bullying or victimization, or both, based on significant odds ratios computed by the authors for the meta-analysis. Be-Prox yielded the highest odds ratio (3.14) in regard to reducing victimization.[28]

## Conclusion

Our findings and those in Farrington and Ttofi's meta-analysis confirm that Be-Prox works and that it is possible to conduct bullying prevention in kindergarten.[29] Changes in teachers' attitudes toward victimized children, the fact that they had gained confidence in handling bullying, and several positive changes in children's reactions in the presence of bullying all offer hope that these teachers will continue acting to prevent bullying or to stop it before an intricate bully-victim pattern can develop.[30] In the meantime, our program has also been used on many occasions with elementary school teachers and even in secondary schools.

## Notes

1. Cook, C. R., Williams, K. R., Guerra, N. G., Kim, T. E., & Sadek, S. (2010). Predictors of bullying and victimization in childhood and adolescence: A meta-analytic investigation. *School Psychology Quarterly, 25*, 65–83.

2. Alsaker, F. D. (2003). *Quälgeister und ihre Opfer. Mobbing unter Kindern— und wie man damit umgeht.* Bern: Huber Verlag; Alsaker, F. D., & Valkanover, S. (2001). Early diagnosis and prevention of victimization in kindergarten. In J. Juvonen & S. Graham (Eds.), *Peer harassment in school: the plight of the vulnerable and victimized* (pp. 175–195). New York, NY: Guilford Press; Kochenderfer, B. J., & Ladd, G. W. (1996). Peer victimization: Cause or consequence of school maladjustment? *Child Development, 67*, 1305–1317; Monks, C. P., Smith, P. K., & Swettenham, J. (2003). Aggressors, victims, and defenders in preschool: Peer, self-, and teacher reports. *Merrill-Palmer Quarterly, 49*, 453–469.

3. Alsaker, F. D. (1993). Isolement et maltraitance par pairs dans les jardins d'enfants: comment mesurer ces phénomènes et quelles en sont leurs conséquences? *Enfance, 47*(3), 241–260; Alsaker, F. D. (2007). *Pathways to victimization and a multisetting intervention.* Bern: Swiss National Science Foundation.

4. Sharp, S. (1995). How much does bullying hurt? The effects of bullying on the personal well-being and educational progress of secondary-aged students. *Educational and Child Psychology, 12*, 81–88.

5. Siegel, R. S., La Greca, A. M., & Harrison, H. M. (2009). Peer victimization and social anxiety in adolescents: Prospective and reciprocal relationships. *Journal of Youth and Adolescence, 38*, 1096–1109.

6. Hanish, L. D., & Guerra, N. G. (2002). A longitudinal analysis of patterns of adjustment following peer victimization. *Development and Psychopathology, 14*, 69–89; Hawker, D.S.J., & Boulton, M. J. (2000). Twenty years' research on peer victimization and psychosocial maladjustment: A meta-analytic review of cross-sectional studies. *Journal of Child Psychology and Psychiatry, 41*, 441–455; Stassen Berger, K. (2007). Update on bullying at school: Science forgotten? *Developmental Review, 27*, 90–126; Alsaker, F. D., & Nägele, C. (2008). Bullying in kindergarten and prevention. In W. Craig & D. Pepler (Eds.), *An international perspective on understanding and addressing bullying* (pp. 230–252). Kingston, Canada: PREVNet; Perren, S. A., & Alsaker F. D. (2009). Depressive symptoms from kindergarten to early school age: Longitudinal associations with social skills deficits and peer victimization. *Child and Adolescent Psychiatry and Mental Health, 3*, 28. www.capmh.com/content/3/1/28.

7. Snyder, J., Brooker, M., Patrick, M. R., Snyder, A., Schrepferman, L., & Stoolmiller, M. (2003). Observed peer victimization during early elementary school: Continuity, growth, and relation to risk for child antisocial and depressive behavior. *Child Development, 74*, 1881–1898.

8. Hauser, D., Gutzwiller-Helfenfinger, E., & Alsaker, F. D. (2009). Kindergartenkinder als Zeugen von Mobbing. *Schweizerische Zeitschrift für Bildungsforschung, 31*(1), 57–74.

9. Alsaker, F. D., & Olweus, D. (2002). Stability and change in global self-esteem and self-related affect. In T. M. Brinthaupt & R. P. Lipka (Eds.),

*Understanding early adolescent self and identity: Applications and interventions* (pp. 193–223). Albany, NY: State University of New York Press.

10. Alsaker, F. D. (2004). The Bernese program against victimization in kindergarten and elementary school (Be-Prox). In P. K. Smith, D. Pepler, & K. Rigby (Eds.), *Bullying in schools: How successful can interventions be?* (pp. 289–306). Cambridge: Cambridge University Press.

11. Alsaker & Valkanover. (2001); Olweus, D. (1993). *Bullying at school. What we know and what we can do.* Oxford: Blackwell; Sharp, S., & Smith, P. K. (1993). Tackling bullying: The Sheffield Project. In D. Tattum (Ed.), *Understanding and managing bullying* (pp. 45–56). London: Heinemann.

12. Rigby, K., Smith, P. K., & Pepler, D. (2004). Working to prevent school bullying: Key issues. In P. K. Smith, D. Pepler, & K. Rigby (Eds.), *Bullying in schools. How successful can interventions be?* (pp. 1–12). Cambridge: Cambridge University Press; Salmivalli, C. (2001). Group view on victimization. In J. Juvonen & S. Graham (Eds.), *Peer harassment in school. The plight of the vulnerable and victimized* (pp. 398–419). New York, NY: Guilford press.

13. Alsaker, F. D. (2012). *Mutig gegen Mobbing in Kindergarten und Schule.* Bern: Huber Verlag.

14. Alsaker. (2003); Roberts, W. B., Jr. (2008). *Working with parents of bullies and victims.* Thousand Oaks, CA: Corwin Press.

15. Snyder et al. (2003).

16. Alsaker. (2004).

17. Gini, G. (2006). Social cognition and moral cognition in bullying: What's wrong? *Aggressive Behavior, 32,* 528–539; Hymel, S., Schonert-Reichl, K. A., Bonanno, R. A., Vaillancourt, T., & Henderson, N. R. (2010). Bullying and morality: Understanding how good kids can behave badly. In S. R. Jimerson, S. M. Swearer, & D. Espelage (Eds.), *The handbook of school bullying. An international perspective* (pp. 101–118). Mahwah, NJ: Erlbaum.

18. Battistich, V., Solomon, D., Watson, D., Solomon, J., & Schaps, E. (1989). Effects of an elementary school program to enhance prosocial behavior on children's cognitive-social problem-solving skills and strategies. *Journal of Applied Developmental Psychology, 10,* 147–169; Bierman, K. L., Greenberg, M. T., & Group, C.P.P.R. (1996). Social skills training in the FAST Track Program. In R. Peters & R. J. McMahon (Eds.), *Preventing childhood disorders, substance abuse, and delinquency* (pp. 65–89). Thousand Oaks, CA: Sage; Smith, P. K., Cowie, H., & Sharp, S. (1994). Working directly with pupils involved in bullying situations. In P. K. Smith & S. Sharp (Eds.), *School bullying: Insights and perspectives* (pp. 193–212). London: Routledge.

19. Alsaker. (2004).

20. Alsaker. (2004).

21. Alsaker. (2004).

22. Valkanover, S. (2005). *Intrigenspiel und Muskelkraft. Aspekte der Psychomotorik im Zusammenhang mit Mobbing im Kindergarten.* Bern: Haupt Verlag.

23. Alsaker. (2004); Alasker & Valkanover. (2001).

24. Alsaker & Valkanover. (2001).

25. Alsaker & Valkanover. (2001).

26. Alsaker. (2003); Alsaker & Valkanover. (2001).

27. Alsaker. (2003).
28. Farrington, D. P., & Ttofi, M. M. (2009). School-based programs to reduce bullying and victimization. *Campbell Systematic Reviews*, 2009, 6. http://www.campbellcollaboration.org/news_/reduction_bullying_schools.php.
29. Farrington & Ttofi. (2009).
30. Alsaker & Nägele. (2008).

FRANÇOISE D. ALSAKER *is a professor in developmental psychology at the University of Berne, Switzerland.*

STEFAN VALKANOVER *is a senior lecturer in sport pedagogy at the University of Berne, Switzerland.*

*Zero tolerance and competent classroom management are key elements in preventing bullying. The Zero program in Norway not only implements a zero vision, but also contains measures to improve teachers' classroom leadership competencies.*

# 3

# The Zero program

## *Erling Roland, Unni Vere Midthassel*

THE ZERO PROGRAM against bullying has a whole-school approach and lasts for approximately sixteen months, including a preparation period from March to the summer vacation in June. It starts by setting up a project group, which the principal leads. In addition, the project group comprises key staff, parents, and students. During spring, this group, with external support from the program owner, prepares the activities for the next school year, when students are exposed to the program.

The development of Zero is closely tied to Norway's work against school bullying, which dates back to 1983. Newspapers then wrote about two youths who committed suicide caused by bullying, and the national minister of education was challenged to do something at a national level. To prepare a national initiative, the minister set up a small committee of two researchers, Dan Olweus and Erling Roland, who were invited to write a book on the topic.[1] Both the Zero and the Olweus program against bullying are clearly rooted in this first national initiative in Norway.[2] The Olweus program lasts for a slightly longer period than Zero and is not as focused as Zero on classroom management. Rather it is

NEW DIRECTIONS FOR YOUTH DEVELOPMENT, NO. 133, SPRING 2012 © WILEY PERIODICALS, INC.
Published online in Wiley Online Library (wileyonlinelibrary.com) • DOI: 10.1002/yd.20005

more focused on direct prevention by discussions with the pupils about bullying.[3]

A definition of bullying, which has since become an international standard, was presented in this book.[4] According to this definition bullying has three elements: (1) negative actions, (2) performed over time by one or several children together, (3) against one who cannot defend himself or herself. Olweus and Roland also wrote the screenplay for the film *Bullying: Scenes from Children's Lives*.[5] This material and national support comprised the national effort, starting in autumn 1983, to combat bullying in Norwegian schools.[6]

The Centre for Behavioural Research (CBR) at Norway's University of Stavanger has carried on the long-term work of developing Zero, although the antibullying approach of the center was not called Zero until 2003. Before that, the ministry gave CBR responsibility for the second national effort, in 1996 and 1997, to combat school bullying. Among the material developed for that effort was a new book that was updated when the Zero program was launched in 2003.[7] The name *Zero* is a direct response to the Norwegian Manifesto Against Bullying announced by the prime minister and central national stakeholders in 2002 in which zero tolerance against bullying was a key approach.[8] Again the ministry asked CBR to assist.

The material from 1996 was reviewed, updated, and expanded. Now, greater emphasis was also laid on schools' commitment in the implementation, implementation support to the schools was strengthened, and the program was named Zero. Since 2003, more than 370 Norwegian schools have carried out the Zero program.

## Zero program content

The Zero program is based on the understanding that bullying is repeated aggressive acts by one (or a few together) and directed at someone who cannot defend himself or herself.[9] Zero emphasizes that bullying can be direct, with punching and kicking, negative words and gestures, and exclusion, or indirect, by spreading false rumors and other manipulation of relations. Digital tools such as cell phones and the Internet can be used as a medium. Bullying may be open but also hidden. Often there are more or less active bystanders. Zero highlights the dynamics of bullying in a social system.[10]

Zero emphasizes that bullying is primarily a proactive aggression.[11] Roland and Idsøe revealed that the main rewards in aggression are power over a vulnerable and helpless victim and increased affiliation with co-bullies as the victim is established as a common disliked person.

This understanding of the central dynamics in bullying makes the rationale for improved classroom leadership an important element of Zero. This rationale is that weak classroom leadership gives room for potential bullies to take negative control in class by exercising power over the teacher and classmates. Weak classroom leadership is also related to the affiliation dynamics by creating social tension among students, which gives potential bullies room to create in-groups by defining external opponents—the victims.[12] Consequently, weak teacher control and support in class can give rise to bullying, while an authoritative teacher, who is strong in both control and support, reduces bullying. Through the program, the entire school staff is trained in setting a standard for a classroom environment that serves as a protection against bullying and in exercising authoritative classroom leadership to achieve this standard. In Zero, this is referred to as *general prevention*.

Bullying-focused prevention builds on good general prevention. The teachers and other staff will have a direct focus on bullying by setting up class rules with students to make them aware of their behavior and to teach them how to understand what bullying is and why it is important to stop it. The role of the bystander and the importance of telling adults are emphasized.

Students play an important role in the behavior that takes place in a group.[13] Nevertheless, in the Zero program, it is the adults who are responsible for setting standards for prevention and intervention.

Zero emphasizes that no matter how good prevention is, bullying episodes will occur. Therefore, teachers need to have the skills to conduct problem-solving conversations in a productive and respectful way. In Zero, all staff are trained to do this.[14] It is recommended that the form teacher (the main teacher of the class) conduct the intervention, eventually supported by other staff, for example, another teacher.

One or more meetings with the victim come first, and they are comforting to and supportive of the child, as it is important that the victim feels certain that the teacher will handle the situation. The teacher ensures the victim that she or he will be informed of each new step in the intervention before it happens. If the victim's parents are not already involved, they are contacted after the first meeting with the victim.

The first meeting with the bully is short and confronting but respectful. If possible, the teacher invites the bully to start being supportive toward the victim. If there is more than one bully, the teacher talks with each child alone without giving the bullies the opportunity to talk to each other between the meetings. Directly after, there is a meeting with all the bullies. They are informed that the bullying must stop immediately and what they may have agreed to do for the person they have bullied. The students are informed that their parents will be contacted the same day; information and contact with parents of the bullies also is part of the intervention.[15]

The teacher follows up with both the victim and the bullies through separate meetings over time. If conditions allow it, the teacher can hold a meeting with both the bully and the victim. Sometimes the parents of both children are present. These meetings between the parties, however, are not a mediation model to stop the bullying; rather, they are the resilience element of Zero. By this we mean how Zero tries to take care of the children after the intervention.

The Zero program is thus a system-oriented effort for an inclusive learning environment focusing on staff development, authoritative classroom leadership as general prevention, bullying-focused prevention, intervention, and resilience.

## Implementation strategy

This program is based on a system-ecological understanding.[16] In the Zero program, all the adults in the school must understand and practice the same standard. To increase their ownership of the antibullying work, all staff are involved in developing an action plan against bullying describing procedures and standards for prevention, detection, and problem solving.[17] The school's student council is involved in efforts to enhance the standard of the environment. Parents are important to students, and research has shown that they affect students' bullying behavior.[18] Parents are engaged in prevention and encouraged to tell the teacher if they have suspicions of bullying.

Zero is given to a cluster of schools, normally three from the same city, town, or community, that work together, and all seminars are common. At each school the principal plays a key role in leading the work with a project group consisting of key teachers, two parents, and two students. An implementation seminar with these project groups starts the work in the spring. Just before school starts after summer vacation, the staff at the schools in the cluster receive a one-day seminar about bullying—its dynamics, prevention, and intervention. In addition, the project groups attend three seminars during the school year. The last seminar, focusing on the continuation after the program period, comes early in the autumn in the next school year. The schools receive materials such as books, films, posters, and presentations for meetings with parents and reflective vests to use in the school yard. The reflective vests are used by the teachers who look after the pupils during breaks. It is supposed that vests symbolize teacher authority and that the vests make the teachers more visible. In spring, before the program begins, students answer a questionnaire about bullying to establish the baseline. This survey is repeated one year later.

The results from these surveys are discussed with staff and parents.

## Research on the Zero program

Research presenting results from the first year of the Zero program included 146 primary schools and over twenty thousand students.[19] The students responded to a questionnaire before the intervention in spring 2003 with an equivalent follow-up in spring 2004. Control data were taken from the national representative School Environment Survey for grades (a grade is equivalent to a form) 5 to 7 in 2001 and 2004, conducted by CBR. The results showed a significant decrease in bullying for Zero schools, and it was greater for grades 5 to 7 than for grades 2 to 4.[20] At control schools, results showed a similar decline for the period 2001 to 2004. The decline in the control schools can be understood in the light of the Norwegian Manifesto Against Bullying, launched by the government and several national stakeholders in 2002, and the implementation of section 9a in the 2003 Education Act. The school environment survey in 2004 showed that 48 percent of schools had intensified efforts to combat bullying in the school year 2001–2002, 58 percent had intensified efforts in the school year 2002–2003, and 79 percent felt that they had intensified the work in the school year 2003–2004. Key elements from Zero or the Olweus program were adopted by the Norwegian schools for this intensified antibullying work during the manifesto period.[21]

In Ireland, the 1996 version of the Zero program was slightly modified to meet cultural differences from the Norwegian context and implemented at forty-two primary schools in County Donegal. The prevalence of victims and bullies involved in bullying weekly or more often was reduced by 30 to 50 percent.[22]

The potential of the Zero program was demonstrated in one Norwegian community in which all six primary schools, quite large ones, participated. Here the prevalence of victims and bullies involved in bullying weekly or more often was reduced between 40 and 70 percent.[23] This demonstrates not only the potential of the program but also the challenge of implementation.

## Research related to program implementation

A qualitative study of the implementation process of the six schools in 2003–2004 revealed some of the challenges schools faced. The first challenge was how prepared schools were to start the work—that is, their readiness. It turned out that schools that could be characterized as mature, ready, and with a clear and firm leadership fared the best with implementation. The role of the school leadership was shown to have two dimensions: "Having a plan and following it, and building structures into the organization with follow-up procedures so that the anti-bullying work is integrated into the everyday life of the school."[24]

## Program effects over time

International research shows that systematic work against bullying through programs is a challenge.[25] In a follow-up study of seventy-two schools that implemented the Zero program, we studied the amount of bullying two years after the program had ended. During these two years, some schools received a follow-up. Twenty-two schools received eight lessons for staff development dealing with central themes in bullying. The same number of schools received phone calls in addition to written material. Twenty-eight schools received no follow-up other than the student surveys that were conducted each year.[26] The results showed that the positive trend that was achieved through the program period remained throughout the two years thereafter for all groups.

There was also a slight but significant decrease in bullying others during the follow-up period. But our assumption that the development would be different for the three groups was not met. All of the schools had developed action plans during the program period, and it is possible that the systematic work was continued in all schools. Furthermore, based on another Norwegian study, it is possible that the weight placed on classroom leadership is a motivation to continue the work because it hits the core competence of being a good teacher.[27] This may be a reason that follow-up was not critical. This calls for further research.

## The way forward

Norwegian authorities have demonstrated concern for school bullying for a long time, and much work has been done by researchers and many schools. The CBR surveys in 2001 and 2004 showed a decline of about 30 percent in victims and bullies and very much suggests that the national Manifesto Against Bullying contributed to this positive development. Our latest survey, in 2008, however, registered a strong increase of about 70 percent in bullying since 2004. The reason might be driven by factors outside the schools. Cyberbullying appears to be the cause of this increase.[28] In addition, a particularly vulnerable group of students has been identified. A recently published research article on bullying among tenth graders related to sexual orientation showed that the proportion of victims among bisexual and homosexual students in particular was dramatically higher than among heterosexual students.[29] Even more surprising was that the percentage of bullies was much higher among bisexual and, especially, homosexual students. The impact was highest for boys as both the harassed and harassers.

Norwegian and international research has brought out a lot about bullying causes, mechanisms, prevention, and responses. A major challenge is to transfer this knowledge to those who need it most. Zero is an example of such a transfer of research-based knowledge to the school system in the form of materials and support from outside. CBR is working to develop and adapt new knowledge in the program and help schools uncover and stop bullying, and eventually prevent it. The work against bullying is not accomplished with a single program or a campaign. It requires systematic work every day in all meetings between students, pupils, and staff. It requires ongoing work for an inclusive learning environment. Then an ecological approach is necessary. We must reach everyone in the organization and the parents. Although parents are outside the organization, they have a great influence on their children and thus relationships among students.[30]

School staff need to develop expertise on how they can be authoritative adults who lead classes and relationship building among students.[31] They need knowledge about how they reveal the social power constellations in the class and what they can do to influence these in a positive direction.[32] They must know how to support students emotionally and professionally so that students will trust them. It is also necessary to have a willingness to see, to care, and to act, and the teachers have to be confident of support from their leadership and colleagues. Therefore, it is necessary for the staff to discuss challenges and learn skills for observation and communication. The schools also need written procedures that tell staff how to prevent, detect, and act when something is uncovered, and it must be clear who is responsible for what. All schools need such an ongoing system-oriented work.

In Norway, the government has recently signed a new manifesto against bullying, and the minister of education has officially declared that ministerial support of antibullying programs, both Zero and other ones, will be an important part of a national strategy. How this strategy will be designed, how the communities and schools respond, and what results they bring remain to be seen.

### Notes

1. Olweus, D., & Roland, E. (1983). *Mobbing—bakgrunn og tiltak*. Oslo: Kirke- undervisnings-og forskningsdepartementet.

2. Olweus, D. (1993). *Bullying at school: What we know and what we can do*. Oxford: Blackwell.

3. Olweus, D. (2005). A useful evaluation design, and effects of the Olweus bullying prevention program. *Psychology, Crime and Law, 11*(4), 389–402.

4. Smith, P. K., Pepler, D., & Rigby, K. (Eds.). (2004). *Bullying in schools: How successful can interventions be?* Cambridge: Cambridge University Press.

5. Olweus & Roland. (1983).

6. Olweus. (2005).

7. Roland, E., & Vaaland, G. S. (1996). *Mobbing i skolen. En lærerveiledning.* Oslo: Kirke- Undervisnings- og Forskningsdepartementet; Roland, E., & Vaaland, G. S. (2003). *Zero, SAFs program mot mobbing.* Stavanger: Senter for atferdsforskning, høgskolen i Stavanger.

8. Roland, E., Bru, E., Midthassel, U. V., & Vaaland, G. S. (2009). The Zero programme against bullying: Effects of the programme in the context of the Norwegian manifesto against bullying. *Social Psychology of Education, 13*(1), 41–55.

9. Olweus & Roland. (1983); Roland & Vaaland. (2003).

10. Roland, E. (2007). *Mobbingens psykologi.* Oslo: Universitetsforlaget; Roland & Vaaland. (2003); Dodge, K. A. (1991). The structure and function of reactive and proactive aggression. In D. Pepler & K. Rubin (Eds.), *The development and treatment of childhood aggression.* Mahwah, NJ: Erlbaum; Dodge, K. A., & Coie, J. D. (1987). Social-information-prosessing factors in reactive and proactive aggression in children's peer groups. *Journal of Personality and Social Psychology, 53*(6), 1146–1158.

11. Roland, E., & Idsøe, T. (2001). Aggression and bullying. *Aggressive Behavior, 27,* 446–462.

12. Roland, E. (1999). *School influences on bullying.* Stavanger: Rebell forlag; Roland, E., & Galloway, D. (2002). Classroom influences on bullying. *Educational Research, 44*(3), 299–312.

13. Salmivalli, C., Lagerspetz, K. M. J., Björkqvist, K., Kaukiainen, A., & Østerman, K. (1996). Bullying is a group process: Participant roles and their relations to social status within the group. *Aggressive Behavior, 22,* 1–15.

14. Roland & Vaaland. (2003).

15. Roland & Vaaland. (2003).

16. Bronfenbrenner, U., & Morris, P. A. (1998). The ecology of development processes. In W. Damon & R. M. Lerner (Eds.), *Handbook of child psychology: Theoretical models of human development* (5th ed., Vol. 1, pp. 993–1029). Hoboken, NJ: Wiley.

17. Midthassel, U. (2005). *Schools' action plan against bullying: Introduction and templates.* http://www.uis.no/COMMON/WEBCENTER/webcenter.nsf/Dok/B18A2C8BC486EF89C12570D1002A37B4?OpenDocument&Connect = 0&Lang = Norsk.

18. Idsøe, T., Solli, E., & Cosmovici, E. M. (2008). Social psychological processes in family and school: More evidence on their relative etiological significance for bullying behavior. *Aggressive Behavior, 34*(5), 460–474.

19. Roland et al. (2009).

20. Roland et al. (2009).

21. Roland et al. (2009).

22. O'Moore, A. M., & Minton, S. J. (2005). An evaluation of the effectiveness of an anti-bullying programme in primary schools. *Aggressive Behavior, 31*(6), 609–622.

23. Midthassel, U., & Roland, E. (2011). Zero-et program mot mobbing. In U. V. Midthassel, E. Bru, S. K. Ertesvåg, & E. Roland (Eds.), *Tidlig intervensjon og systemrettet arbeid for et godt læringsmiljø.* Oslo: Universitetsforlaget.

24. Midthassel, U., & Ertesvåg, S. (2008). Schools implementing Zero: The process of implementing an antibullying programme in six Norwegian schools. *Journal of Educational Change*, *9*, 153–172.

25. Koivisto, M. (2004). A follow-up survey of anti-bullying interventions in the comprehensive schools of Kempele in 1990–98. In P. K. Smith, D. Pepler, & K. Rigby (Eds.), *Bullying in schools. How successful can interventions be?* (pp. 235–249). Cambridge: Cambridge University Press; Limber, S. P., Nation, M., Tracy, A. J., Melton, G. B., & Flerx, V. (2004). Implementation of the Olweus bullying prevention programme in the southeastern United States. In P. K. Smith, D. Pepler, & K. Rigby (Eds.), *Bullying in schools. How successful can interventions be?* (pp. 55–80). Cambridge: Cambridge University Press; Roland, E., & Galloway, D. (2004). Professional cultures in schools with high and low rates of bullying. *School Effectiveness and School Improvement*, *15*(3–4), 241–260; Roland. (1999).

26. Midthassel, U., Bru, E., & Idsøe, T. (2008). Is the sustainability of reduction in bullying related to follow-up procedures? *Educational Psychology*, *28*(1), 83–95.

27. Midthassel, U., & Bru, E. (2001). Predictors and gains of teacher involvement in an improvement project on classroom management: Experiences from a Norwegian project in two compulsory schools. *Educational Psychology*, *21*(3), 229–242.

28. Roland. (2007).

29. Roland, E., & Auestad, G. (2009). *Seksuell orientering og mobbing*. Stavanger: Universitetet i Stavanger.

30. Idsøe et al. (2008).

31. Roland, E. (1995). *Elevkollektivet*. Stavanger: Rebell forlag.

32. Roland. (1995); Vaaland, G. S. (2007). Høyt spill om samspill. In G. S. Vaaland (Ed.), *Høyt spill om samspill: Å snu vanskelige klasser* (pp. 2–10). Stavanger: Senter for atferdsforskning, Universitetet i Stavanger.

ERLING ROLAND *is a professor in educational psychology at the Centre for Behaviour Research, University of Stavanger, Norway.*

UNNI VERE MIDTHASSEL *is an associate professor and director of the Centre for Behaviour Research, University of Stavanger, Norway.*

*Most bullying incidents happen when peers are present. The KiVa program not only trains teachers, but also contains effective strategies to change bystanders into defenders.*

# 4

# Making bullying prevention a priority in Finnish schools: The KiVa antibullying program

*Christina Salmivalli, Elisa Poskiparta*

AS IN MANY other societies, bullying has been a big concern in Finland for several decades. For many years, there was a persistent belief that the problem could be tackled by legislative changes (requiring schools to develop their own action plans against bullying) or by a commitment of school personnel to intervene immediately whenever they see bullying taking place (zero tolerance). It seems, however, that adults working in schools need more concrete tools for bullying prevention work with children and youth, just as they need clear guidelines to intervene when bullying is detected. It is not enough to do something: there is now a rich body of evidence on the mechanisms of bullying, and this knowledge must be incorporated in antibullying measures in order for them to be effective.

In 2006, the Finnish Ministry of Education and Culture contracted with the University of Turku concerning the development and evaluation of an antibullying program that could be implemented widely in Finnish comprehensive schools. The program,

NEW DIRECTIONS FOR YOUTH DEVELOPMENT, NO. 133, SPRING 2012 © WILEY PERIODICALS, INC.
Published online in Wiley Online Library (wileyonlinelibrary.com) • DOI: 10.1002/yd.20006

KiVa (an acronym for Kiusaamista Vastaan, "against bullying"; the Finnish adjective *kiva* also means "nice"), was developed and evaluated at the University of Turku, in collaboration between the Department of Psychology and the Centre for Learning Research. The KiVa program was developed for schools providing comprehensive education (grades 1 to 9 in the Finnish school system, with students between about seven and fifteen years old). The first phase of the KiVa project (from 2006 to 2009) included the development of the program (three versions for different grade levels), training school personnel during the piloting period, and a large-scale evaluation study. The diffusion of the KiVa program in Finnish schools at large started in 2009, and about 82 percent of Finnish comprehensive schools are implementing it now. This article provides an overview of the KiVa antibullying program and its implementation and reviews findings concerning its effectiveness.

## *Research background and goals of KiVa*

The KiVa antibullying program is well grounded in research. It is based on decades of research done by our group in Finland and other researchers from around the world. The program is predicated on the idea that how peer bystanders, who are neither bullies nor victims, react when witnessing bullying is crucial for either maintaining bullying or putting an end to it.

Unlike many antisocial acts such as shoplifting or substance use, in which youth engage mostly in their free time together with their friends, much of the bullying takes place on school playgrounds and is witnessed by relatively large audiences of peers.[1] Unfortunately, peer witnesses often behave in ways that encourage the bully and provide social rewards to him or her rather than taking sides with the victim.[2] Reinforcement of the bully may involve displays of approval (smiling, laughing along) or direct verbal incitements.[3] Even subtle positive feedback by nonverbal cues can be rewarding for the children doing the bullying. Apart from bullying incidents as such, it might become normative in the peer group to treat the victimized child in a mean way; it is perceived "normal" that he or she is excluded from activities, constantly laughed at, or just ignored. Even if most children and youth think that bullying is wrong, they rarely express such private attitudes in public, especially when the perpetrator of bullying is a high-status peer.

The bystanders' behaviors carry consequences for the targets of bullying, as well as for the children engaging in bullying. For the targets, the most painful experience involved in being bullied is not necessarily the attacks by one or two mean kids, but the perception that the whole group is against them: no one seems to care about their pain. Research evidence shows that victims who are supported or defended even by a single classmate are less depressed and anxious, have higher self-esteem, and are less rejected by their peers than victims without defenders.[4]

When others do nothing to support the victim or laugh when bullying occurs, they socially reward those doing the bullying, who are more likely to continue their mean acts. It has been demonstrated that bullying behavior occurs more frequently in classrooms where reinforcing is common and few children take sides with the victims.[5] Furthermore, individual risk factors such as social anxiety are more likely to be associated with victimization in classrooms where reinforcing the bully is normative.[6]

An important message from these studies is that in order to reduce victimization, it is not necessary to somehow make the victims "less vulnerable." And the behavior of the aggressive bullies might be difficult to change directly if the peer context is ignored: the perpetrators of bullying are often successful in gaining prestige.[7] Influencing the behaviors of classmates can reduce the social rewards that the bullies gain and, consequently, their motivation to bully in the first place.

Researchers in the field now share the view that influencing peer bystanders is a key to effective and sustainable bullying interventions.[8] In the KiVa antibullying program, this idea is translated into concrete tools that help adults, and children and youth themselves, to tackle bullying in a systematic way.

## Program elements and implementation model

The aims of the KiVa antibullying program are to put an end to ongoing bullying, prevent the emergence of new bully-victim relationships, and minimize the negative consequences of victimization. The focus is on influencing the peer bystanders, who are neither bullies nor victims, to make them show that they are against bullying and to make them support the victim rather than encourage the bully.

KiVa is a whole-school program and thus requires the commitment of all personnel. KiVa is not meant to be a project that lasts for a certain period of time and then ends. It is meant to become part of the school's ongoing antibullying efforts. Table 4.1 provides an overview of the implementation of the KiVa program during one school year (in Finland, from mid-August to the end of May).

KiVa involves several universal actions, such as student lessons (primary school) and themes containing several lessons (secondary school), accompanied by virtual learning environments that are closely connected to their contents. During the evaluation study (a randomized controlled trial) of KiVa, the three versions of KiVa student lessons and themes were delivered in grades 1 to 3, 4 to 6, and 7 to 9. For continuing implementation of KiVa, we recommend that at the primary school level, student lessons are delivered in the first and fourth grades. There are ten double lessons (a double lesson lasts ninety minutes) for both of these grade levels. In lower secondary and middle school, the four themes are recommended to be targeted at seventh graders. A student in a KiVa school will thus attend the lessons and themes three times during his or her compulsory education: first at the beginning of the school career, then in grade 4, and for the last time in grade 7, right after the middle school transition.

The lessons and themes, carried out by the classroom teacher, involve discussion, group work, short films about bullying, and role-play exercises. The contents of the lessons proceed from more general topics, such as emotions, the importance of respect in

## Table 4.1. Implementation of the KiVa antibullying program during one school year

| Month | Staff | Students | Parents | All cases of bullying coming to attention |
|---|---|---|---|---|
| August | Staff meeting | Kick-off (all students), lesson 1 (grades 1 and 4) | Newsletters to homes | Immediate response to bullying cases and follow-up (KiVa team plus classroom teacher) |
| September | | Lesson 2 (grades 1 and 4), theme 1 (grade 7) | Back-to-school night for parents | |
| October | | Lesson 3 (grades 1 and 4) | | |
| November | | Lesson 4 (grades 1 and 4), theme 2 (grade 7) | | |
| December | | Lesson 5 (grades 1 and 4) | | |
| January | | Lesson 6 (grades 1 and 4), theme 3 (grade 7) | | |
| February | | Lesson 7 (grades 1 and 4) | | |
| March | | Lesson 8 (grades 1 and 4), theme 4 (grade 7) | | |
| April | | Lesson 9 (grades 1 and 4) | | |
| May | | Lesson 10 (grades 1 and 4), KiVa student survey (all grades) | | |

NEW DIRECTIONS FOR YOUTH DEVELOPMENT • DOI: 10.1002/yd

relationships, and group pressure, to bullying and its mechanisms and consequences. Several lessons (themes) concern the role of the group in either maintaining bullying or putting an end to it. The group exercises involve, among other things, brainstorming ways to support and help the bullied victims and practicing these skills. Studies have shown that empathy toward the victimized peers, as well as self-efficacy to defend and support them, are important characteristics that should be promoted if we want to make defending more common.[9] The lessons and themes are accompanied with virtual learning environments, that is, antibullying computer games for grades 1 and 4 and an online environment called "KiVa Street" for grade 7. Their purpose is to motivate students and enhance their learning process.

We believe that specific actions are also needed to tackle the cases of bullying that come to the attention of school personnel. In KiVa, the indicated actions are effectuated by school KiVa teams, together with classroom teachers. The KiVa team consists of three teachers (or other school personnel) in each participating school, whose main task is to tackle, with the classroom teachers, the cases of bullying that come to their attention. This happens through a set of individual and group discussions that one or two team members go through with the victim and with the bullies and systematic follow-up meetings. In addition to these discussions, the classroom teacher arranges a meeting with two to four selected classmates in order to encourage them to support the victimized child. The teacher manuals include detailed guidelines about how the discussions are carried through.

To make KiVa visible for all students and personnel in the school, the program materials include highly visible vests for teachers who are monitoring recess. The highly visible vests signal that bullying is taken seriously in the school. There are also posters that can be hung on classroom or school corridor walls to remind everyone about KiVa. For parents, an information leaflet is sent to each home at the beginning of the school year, presentation slides are used at back-to-school night for parents, and a parents' Web site provides information about bullying and advice concerning what parents can do to help reduce the problem or even prevent it.

Before the beginning of implementation, school personnel are provided with two days of face-to-face training. Those participating in the training then pass on to others in their school what they have learned. The recommended time for face-to-face training is the spring term preceding implementation, which begins in the fall. In addition to face-to-face training, KiVa offers an online training package for those who were unable to participate in the face-to-face training, new personnel in schools already implementing KiVa, and new schools adopting the program. The online training content is similar to that of the face-to-face training. The KiVa Web site also has a discussion forum where personnel of KiVa schools can share ideas, experiences, and challenges concerning program implementation.

There is an annual online survey to be filled out by the students and personnel of KiVa schools, providing feedback to schools regarding their situation (for example, the prevalence of bullied students and their perpetrators) and their level of implementation of the KiVa program. Thus, schools can compare their situation to previous years, as well as to the situation of other schools. Students respond to the survey for the first time in the spring preceding implementation and then at the same time every year. School personnel start answering the survey after the first year of implementation.

Good coordination is essential. Therefore, each school should appoint a person in charge of the implementation of KiVa. She or he is familiarized with the program as a whole, coordinates the implementation, and assists when needed in other matters related to the program. In the fall when implementation begins, schools organize their own staff meeting where everyone is informed about KiVa, and there is a kick-off session for all students. Newsletters are sent to KiVa schools four times a year with reminders about important aspects of implementation, acknowledging schools for their efforts and serving as a motivator. All registered KiVa schools are provided with quality recommendations—

guidelines that help schools monitor their implementation of the KiVa program. Finally, in 2010, we started organizing biannual KiVa days, a two-day conference where the personnel from KiVa schools can hear about the latest research based on KiVa data, get further training, and share their experiences and outcomes.

Because KiVa includes both preventive and interceptive elements, it works for very different schools and classes and for bullying cases that have emerged recently as well as those that have lasted longer. The preconditions for implementation include personnel who are committed enough to deliver the universal actions and a minimum of three people who are motivated to work on a school team handling the program. The principal's role is important in ensuring resources and providing support for high-quality implementation.[10]

## Evaluation results

Program evaluation was considered a central part of the KiVa project from the beginning. A randomized control design was used to evaluate program effects. Altogether 234 schools representing all provinces in mainland Finland (and both Finnish- and Swedish-speaking schools) were randomly assigned to intervention and control conditions (twenty-eight thousand students were involved).

KiVa data are longitudinal, containing three assessment points during a one-year period: the pretest, the evaluation after five months of intervention, and the evaluation after nine to ten months of intervention. At each assessment, students logged in to the Web-based questionnaire (developed specifically for the KiVa project) using their passwords. Thus, individual students, as well as whole classrooms and schools, could be followed over time. In addition, we have continued a follow-up of one cohort (children who were in the fourth grade during the first phase of program evaluation in 2007–2008) in order to examine the long-term psychosocial and academic adjustment of victims and bullies who remained in their roles despite the KiVa intervention versus those who benefited from the intervention.

KiVa data are unique not only in the number of participants but also in the wealth of factors assessed. Besides bullying and victimization, the data contain information about children's and adolescents' family structure, possible immigrant status, school and class atmosphere, school motivation and well-being, learning outcomes, peer acceptance and rejection, friendships, peer networks, self-esteem and generalized perception of peers, and social-emotional problems such as social anxiety, depression, and loneliness. Self-reports, peer reports, and dyadic questions are used.

Besides student questionnaires, teacher reports regarding their attitudes, self-efficacy, and efforts to tackle bullying, as well as information regarding their students (for example, about learning difficulties and special educational needs), have been collected. Furthermore, teachers have provided us with detailed data on the implementation of the KiVa program, enabling us to study how the implementation varies across schools, which teacher- and school-related factors explain this variation, and how differences in implementation are reflected in program effects.

The findings from the evaluation studies of KiVa have been reported in numerous empirical studies. The main effects of the program after one school year (nine months) of implementation have been rigorously evaluated, first in a randomized controlled trial and later during the broad nationwide rollout.[11]

In the randomized controlled trial, KiVa was found to reduce bullying and victimization significantly at primary school levels 1 to 6.[12] In grades 7 to 9 the effects were more mixed, and they seemed to depend on gender (larger effects among boys) and the proportion of boys in the classroom, so that even among girls, larger effects were in many cases found in classrooms with higher proportions of boys.[13] The average effect sizes across all grade levels, with odds ratios of 1.28 (victimization) and 1.30 (bullying), are clearly larger than effect sizes from other bullying intervention studies using a similar design (schools randomly assigned to intervention and control conditions). The effects sizes indicate that after being exposed to the KiVa program for nine months, the odds of being a victim or being a bully were about 1.3 times higher for a control school student than for a student in an intervention school. In primary school, the effects were even larger, with the largest effects in grades 3 and 4 (1.58 and 1.83 for victimization and 2.08 and 1.30 for bullying).

During the broad dissemination of KiVa, the effects on bullying and victimization were somewhat smaller than those obtained in the randomized controlled trial, and again they varied across grade levels, being largest in grade 4 and smallest in middle school (grades 7 to 9).[14] It should be noted, however, that all effects reported so far have been obtained after only one school year (nine months) of implementation. The data from the annual student surveys from schools implementing KiVa will be used to study the effects of the program when more time has been devoted to implementation.

Besides the positive effects on bullying and victimization, KiVa has been shown to increase school liking, academic motivation, and even academic performance among students in KiVa schools as compared to students from control schools.[15] Furthermore, KiVa reduces internalizing problems and negative peer perceptions and increases empathy, self-efficacy to defend the victimized peers, and constructive bystander behaviors.[16] We were also impressed to discover that children who were victimized by their peers played in the online KiVa game even more often both in and out of the school compared with bullies and noninvolved students.[17]

The outcomes of the indicated actions, that is, discussions effectuated by KiVa teams, have been evaluated in a separate study.[18] From among all cases that were tackled by KiVa teams during the randomized controlled trial, as many as 98 percent led to improvement in the victim's situation, and in 86 percent of the cases, bullying stopped completely, as reported by (former) victims in the follow-up discussions. The problem seems to be that most targets of systematic bullying still do not report their harassment at school or at home, thus hindering effective intervention. To foster reporting to adults, we have added a new feature to antibullying computer games for grades 1 and 4 and online KiVa Street for grade 7: from the next school year on, there is a mailbox that students can use to send e-mail concerning their own victimization or victimization targeted at a peer at school. The message automatically goes to members of the school's KiVa team.

The Finnish school system has a reputation of being highly effective in terms of producing good academic outcomes (http://pisacountry.acer.edu.au). We are, however, even prouder of the fact that the Finnish government wanted to take students' school well-being seriously and decided that preventing bullying was a priority. Overall, the KiVa initiative is an example of how commitment from politicians as well as participating schools can lead to excellent results influencing the lives of numerous children and adolescents. The strong theoretical and empirical base of KiVa leads us to believe that it will work in contexts outside Finland as well.

### Notes

1. Kiesner, J., & Fassetta, E. (2009). Old friends and new friends: Their presence at substance-use initiation. *International Journal of Behavioral Development, 33*, 299–302; Kiesner, J., Poulin, F., & Dishion, T. (2010). Adolescent substance use with friends: Moderating and mediating effects of parental monitoring and peer activity contexts. *Merrill-Palmer Quarterly, 56*, 529–556; Fekkes, M., Pijpers, F., & Verloove-Vanhorick, S. (2005). Bullying: Who does what, when and where? Involvement of children, teachers and parents in bullying behavior. *Health Education Research, 20*, 81–91; Atlas, R. S., & Pepler, D. J. (1998). Observations of bullying in the classroom. *Journal of Educational Research, 92*, 86–99; Craig, W., Pepler, D., & Atlas, R. (2000). Observations of bullying on the playground and in the classroom. *School Psychology International, 21*, 22–36.

2. Craig, W., & Pepler, D. (1997). Observations of bullying and victimization in the schoolyard. *Canadian Journal of School Psychology, 13*, 41–59; Salmivalli, C., Lagerspetz, K., Björkqvist, K., Österman, K., & Kaukiainen, A. (1996). Bullying as a group process: Participant roles and their relations to social status within the group. *Aggressive Behavior, 22*, 1–15; Sutton, J., & Smith, P. K. (1999). Bullying as a group process: An adaptation of the participant role approach. *Aggressive Behavior, 25*, 97–111.

3. Salmivalli, C., & Voeten, M. (2004). Connections between attitudes, group norms, and behaviour in bullying situations. *International Journal of Behavioral Development, 28*, 246–258.

4. Sainio, M., Veenstra, R., Huitsing, G., & Salmivalli, C. (2011). Victims and their defenders: A dyadic approach. *International Journal of Behavioral Development*, *35*, 144–151.

5. Salmivalli, C., Kärnä, A., & Poskiparta, E. (2011). Counteracting bullying in Finland: The KiVa program and its effects on different forms of being bullied. *International Journal for Behavioral Development*, *35*, 405–411.

6. Kärnä, A., Voeten, M., Poskiparta, E., & Salmivalli, C. (2010). Vulnerable children in varying classroom contexts: Bystanders' behaviors moderate the effects of risk factors on victimization. *Merrill-Palmer Quarterly*, *56*, 261–282.

7. Juvonen, J., Graham, S., & Schuster, M. (2003). Bullying among young adolescents: The strong, weak, and troubled. *Pediatrics*, *112*, 1231–1237.

8. Frey, K. S., Hirschstein, M. K., Edström, L. V., & Snell, J. L. (2009). Observed reductions in school bullying, nonbullying aggression, and destructive bystander behavior: A longitudinal evaluation. *Journal of Educational Psychology*, *101*, 466–481; Pepler, D., Craig, W., & O'Connell, P. (2010). Peer processes in bullying: Informing prevention and intervention strategies. In S. R. Jimerson, S. M. Swearer, & D. L. Espelage (Eds.), *Handbook of bullying in schools: An international perspective* (pp. 469–479). New York, NY: Routledge; Salmivalli, C., Kärnä, A., & Poskiparta, E. (2010). From peer putdowns to peer support: A theoretical model and how it translated into a national antibullying program. In S. R. Jimerson, S. M. Swearer, & D. L. Espelage (Eds.), *Handbook of bullying in schools: An international perspective* (pp. 441–454). New York, NY: Routledge.

9. Pöyhönen, V., Juvonen, J., & Salmivalli, C. (2010). What does it take to stand up for the victim of bullying? The interplay between personal and social factors. *Merrill-Palmer Quarterly*, *56*, 143–163.

10. Ahtola, A., Haataja, A., Kärnä, A., Poskiparta, E., & Salmivalli, C. (2011). *Implementation fidelity of a national antibullying program, KiVa: Principal support as a regulator.* Manuscript submitted for publication.

11. Kärnä, A., Voeten, M., Little, T.D., Alanen, E., Poskiparta, E., & Salmivalli, C. (2011a). Effectiveness of the KiVa antibullying program: Grades 1–3 and 7–9. Manuscript submitted for publication; Kärnä, A., Voeten, M., Little, T., Poskiparta, E., Kaljonen, A., & Salmivalli, C. (2011). A large-scale evaluation of the KiVa antibullying program: Grades 4–6. *Child Development*, *82*(1), 311–330.; Kärnä, A., Voeten, M., Little, T.D., Poskiparta, E., Alanen, E., & Salmivalli, C. (2011b). Going to scale: A nonrandomized nationwide trial of the KiVa antibullying program for Grades 1–9. *Journal of Consulting and Clinical Psychology*, *79*, 796–805.

12. Kärnä et al. (2011a).

13. Kärnä et al. (2011b).

14. Kärnä et al. (2011b).

15. Salmivalli, C., Garandeau, C., & Veenstra, R. (2012). KiVa antibullying program: Implications for school adjustment. In G. Ladd & A. Ryan (Eds.), *Peer relationships and adjustment at school* (pp. 279–307). Charlotte, NC: Information Age Publishing.

16. Williford, A., Boulton, A., Noland, B., Kärnä, A., Little, T., & Salmivalli, C. (2011). Effects of the KiVa antibullying program on adolescents' perception of peers, depression, and anxiety. *Journal of Abnormal Child Psychology*, *40*, 289–300.

17. Poskiparta, E., Kaukiainen, A., Pöyhönen, V., & Salmivalli, C. (2012). Anti-bullying computer game as part of the KiVa program: Students' perceptions of the game. In A. Costabile & B. Spears (Eds.), *The impact of technology on relationships in educational settings: International Perspectives* (pp. 158–168). New York, NY: Routledge.

18. Garandeau, C. F., Little, T., Kärnä, A., Poskiparta, E., & Salmivalli, C. (2011, August). *Dealing with bullies at school: Which approach for which situations?* Paper presented at the Biennial Meeting of the European Society for Developmental Psychology, Bergen, Norway.

CHRISTINA SALMIVALLI *is a professor of psychology at the University of Turku and director of the KiVa antibullying program.*

ELISA POSKIPARTA *is a special researcher and leader of the Center for Learning Research at the University of Turku, and director of the KiVa antibullying program.*

*Effective preventive intervention programs target-ing bullying and relational aggression view bully-ing and relational aggression as a peer group phenomenon.*

# 5

# School-based prevention of bullying and relational aggression in adolescence: The fairplayer.manual

*Herbert Scheithauer, Markus Hess,*
*Anja Schultze-Krumbholz, Heike Dele Bull*

BULLYING IS LONG-TERM repeated victimization with an imbalance of power between the bully and victim.[1] It can be verbal, physical, or psychological (relational) in nature. *Relational aggression* refers to harmful behaviors (such as social exclusion or gossip) that destroy or threaten to destroy social relationships.[2,3] Thus, relational aggression can constitute bullying if it occurs repeatedly over time and if those who are targeted cannot defend themselves against the perpetrator.

Bullying is highly prevalent in the everyday life of many adoles-cents in Germany. For example, in a study of about two thousand adolescents, we found that 12.1 percent of the students reported bullying others and 11.1 percent reported being bullied at least once a week.[4] In addition, cyberbullying, that is, bullying others using modern forms of communication, is a problem at German schools, with about 16 percent of students being victims and 17 percent being cyberbullies at least two or three times a month.[5]

NEW DIRECTIONS FOR YOUTH DEVELOPMENT, NO. 133, SPRING 2012 © WILEY PERIODICALS, INC.
Published online in Wiley Online Library (wileyonlinelibrary.com) • DOI: 10.1002/yd.20007

A multitude of studies has revealed negative outcomes or correlates of bullying, such as helplessness, feelings of loneliness,
anxiety disorders, depression, suicide (also referred to as bully-
cide), relationship problems, psychosomatic disorders, eating disorders, or school avoidance and lower academic performance for
the victims, and relationship problems, aggressive and delinquent
behavior, lack of prosocial behavior, dating violence, risk behaviors, or low school bonding for the bullies.[6] Thus, bullying in
schools is a negative behavior accompanied by a multitude of negative consequences for affected students. It is absolutely necessary
to implement appropriate intervention and prevention programs.

## Main theoretical ideas and target groups

Many theories and models explaining bullying in the school context have been offered, including individual (for example, the social
deficit model), school-teacher-parent (learning-theory-oriented
models), school class (for example, deficient class climate), schoolwide and school ethos (lack of participation possibilities for students, lack of adequate school policy), and even integrative
social-ecological approaches.

Often bullying is approached as an individual or dyadic problem
of bully and victim. This approach, however, ignores the social
context of bullying and the presence of peers who are neither the
primary bully nor the victim. According to the participant-role
approach, students take on various roles.[7] Some of them support
the bully through active and clear encouragement (they are
referred to as assistants), others support the bully in a less active
way (reinforcers), passive bystanders (outsiders) tolerate the bullying behavior and are therefore perceived as supportive of the bully
by the victim, and still other children directly express their disap-
proval of the bullying behavior (defenders). We believe that bullying and relational aggression can be reduced or even prevented if
peers act supportively rather than with indifference toward victims. Approving bullying and relational aggressive behavior,

NEW DIRECTIONS FOR YOUTH DEVELOPMENT • DOI: 10.1002/yd

however, can lead to further escalation, affecting social relations, school climate, and peer relations.

A lack of action against bullying is associated with positive attitudes and (group) norms toward bullying, a negative class climate, and low identification with the school and class environment. Several risk factors at the individual level have been identified, for example, being oblivious to bullying behavior and a lack of individual responsibility to intervene, deficits in social-emotional competencies (such as empathy or sympathy), a biased interpretation of social-cognitive cues in social interactions, negative peer status, and a lack of positive social norms that form the basis of prosocial behavior. Finally, many teachers, administrators, and parents ignore, passively support, or even engage in bullying behaviors themselves.[8,9,10] The intervention strategies of the multicomponent preventive intervention program fairplayer.manual cover the three levels that have been considered important in the earlier literature: school/teacher, class/group, and individual student level.[11] The main emphasis, however, is on the group mechanisms of bullying, and therefore, intervening, at the class level (for seventh to ninth graders). Parts of the program can be labeled as universal because they address an entire class and all of its members; other parts of the program can be labeled as selective or indicated prevention because they are designed to address high-risk-group children or causal risk factors, respectively.

## Program elements and implementation model

The aims of the fairplayer.manual are:

- Raising awareness of bullying and/or of relational aggression (negative behavior) and its negative effects and of prosocial (positive) behavior
- Modification of probullying into antibullying attitudes and norms (for example, by increasing a sense of personal

responsibility to intervene, readiness to take action against bullying, proscription of bullying behavior)
- The fostering of positive peer relationships and a positive class climate
- The fostering of social-emotional competencies (such as perspective-taking skills, empathy and sympathy, and adequate social-cognitive perception) and moral sensitivity
- Prevention or a decrease in bullying or relational aggressive behavior, increasing prosocial behavior, helping students to develop alternatives to relational aggression, and supporting the acquisition of adequate strategies to act, or react, in case of bullying

These aims are to be achieved by using several active and interactive methods:

- Awareness raising and attitude change through discussion groups, information, feedback, and role plays
- Cognitive-behavioral methods (model learning, behavioral exercises, implementation of behavioral rules and classwide rules, social reinforcement, feedback)
- Methods to modify students' social-cognitive information processing and foster their social skills (for example, a differentiated perception of social situations, empathy training, structured role plays, behavioral exercises)
- Moral dilemma discussions
- Methods to modify group dynamics: participant role plays such as structured role plays, preparation and enactment of a play, and behavioral exercises in groups.

These methods illustrate that the program's "idea of man" is rooted in social constructivist and social learning theory: that people are active and adaptive, autonomic, with an individual (social) perception of the world, but influenced by experiences within their social environment. The individual has sole responsibility for and actively constructs his or her learning processes.[12] The main message is "to be a fair player" (see Figure 5.1).

**Figure 5.1. Example of publicity materials of the nonprofit, registered organization "fairplayer e.V."**

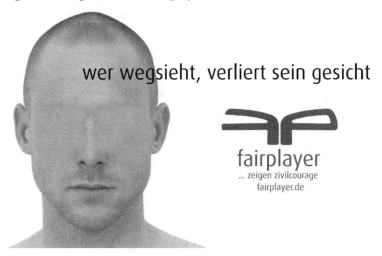

*Note:* The message is, "To look away means to lose face—fair players display civil courage."

The program consists of at least fifteen to seventeen consecutive ninety-minute lessons and is implemented in regular school lessons over four to six months. Following training, teachers or school social workers implement fairplayer.manual together with skilled psychologists, referred to as fairplayer.teamers. We strongly recommend implementing the program as a whole-school approach, not in a single class only, and at least all classes for a single grade, accompanied by a two-day workshop for all of the teachers at the school. Finally, we recommend conducting at least two parents' evenings, before and after program implementation. We also offer materials for parents, such as information about bullying, telephone help lines, and indicators of a child's potential involvement in bullying.

Many programs aiming at reducing bullying seem to work only in the short term because they often take place during a limited period of time and there is no follow-up. The aim of fairplayer. manual is not to be implemented once as a project but rather for teachers to continue using certain measures of the program, integrating them into daily school routines (program sustainability). For this reason, additional measures are planned (see the section "Further development of the program and additional information" at the end of the article).

Teachers attend a several-day training program before program implementation and halfway through implementation. The training includes facilitated discussions, mini-lectures, hands-on exercises, implementation planning, and support after the training. During the training, teachers are provided with facts about bullying, including research findings on bullying and its mechanisms; information about methods of intervening in bullying at the individual, class, and school levels (with an emphasis on class-level interventions); and freedom to discuss and share experiences about effective ways of intervening. Teachers are encouraged to discuss bullying with the whole class, focusing, for example, on group mechanisms and participant roles. Students' experiences, awareness raising, self-reflection, and commitment to antibullying behaviors form the basis of the discussions. Specific examples of working out the participant role theme with the class are introduced to the teachers. Prepared materials for aiding curriculum-based work on the program's measures, such as role plays and role-playing exercises, photos, and films, are introduced during the training. During implementation, we offer at least two group supervision meetings to discuss possible problems and barriers to implementing the program. At any time, teachers can consult the fairplayer.teamer on individual cases they find difficult to deal with.

## Brief summary of evaluation results

It is essential to test the efficacy of intervention programs by comparing the pre- and postdata of students who received the intervention (the intervention group) with those who did not (controls). The evaluation of the program consists of four stages, from a preformative, to a formative, and then a summative stage (see Table 5.1). We started with a pilot study and conducted three evaluation

## Table 5.1. The four independent evaluation studies

| Evaluation studies | Evaluation stages |
|---|---|
| I. Pilot study: $N = 226$ | Conceptual stage (preformative stage): Concept of intervention |
| II. First pilot evaluation study: $N = 113$ | Development stage (formative stage): Pilot study, feasibility, effectiveness |
| III. Second evaluation study: $N = 119$ | Examination stage (first summative stage): Effectiveness study |
| IV. Third evaluation study: $N = 220$ (still ongoing) | Routine stage (second summative stage): Effectiveness study |

studies, each with different aims. The four gender-balanced samples add up to 678 students (562 intervention groups and 116 control groups), with an age range from eleven to nineteen years (some of the samples included fifth graders, others tenth graders and students from vocational schools).

Thus, evaluation data were collected in four independent evaluation studies using standardized instruments (self-report questionnaire, peer nominations and ratings, teacher nominations and ratings, teacher self-reports), which were administered on two or three different occasions: prior to the intervention (pre), after the intervention (post), and in some of the studies some time afterward (follow-up). An overview of administered instruments and evaluation designs can be found in Scheithauer and Bull.[13] Here, we summarize selected results from evaluation studies II and III.

### Evaluation study II

In the study were 138 students , thirteen to twenty-one years old, from comprehensive and vocational schools, and their teachers ($N = 12$).[14] We obtained data on 113 students before and after intervention (shortly following program implementation). Due to a high attrition rate, we were unable to use the information from an initially recruited control group. Results can be summarized as follows:

- Self-reported bullying, measured with the Bully/Victim Questionnaire (BVQ), declined noticeably after program implementation: for bullies from 24 to 19 percent, for victims from 24 to 12 percent, and for bully/victims from 9 to 3 percent.

- Prosocial behavior increased significantly.
- Empathy differed for classes according to treatment integrity—that is the degree to which the intervention has been implemented as intended (a minor increase in classes with higher treatment integrity and a significant decrease in classes with low treatment integrity).
- Legitimation of aggression or violence decreased significantly in classes with higher treatment integrity.

After program implementation, teachers reported an increase of prosocial behavior among their students and a decrease of aggressive behavior, and they described their students as "more reflective" concerning topics like violence or civil courage. However, analyses revealed positive effects in only some of the intervention classes. Heterogeneous evaluation results might be due to the low degree of actual implementation of the program in some of the classes. Typically the extent to which the components of a program are put into practice is up to the schools and teachers involved. Indeed, our findings suggest that the effectiveness (or lack of it) of the intervention program may be due to the implementation process itself because the low intervention effects emerged in classes in which program parts were not fully implemented.

In short, the results of this pilot study partially indicated impressive positive changes concerning the total number of bullies and victims, as well as prosocial behavior. Results concerning legitimation of violence and empathy differed for classes according to treatment integrity.

### Evaluation study III

The gender-balanced sample consisted of 119 adolescents, aged fourteen to seventeen years, from comprehensive schools.[15] We used a controlled pre-, post- (four months later), follow-up (another twelve months later) design, including a long-term (sixteen weeks) and a short-term (ten weeks) intervention group. Participating school classes were not randomized. Results are summarized below:

- The total number of self-reported victims and bullies decreased or did not change meaningfully for both intervention groups but increased in the control group.
- In a multinomial logistic regression analysis, we found no significant change in the number of bullies (self-report) but a significant decrease in the number of victims (self-report) in the short-term intervention group.
- The frequency of self-reported bullying behavior significantly decreased in both of the intervention groups, but not in the control group.
- All effects concerning relational aggression were independent of gender, age, and school class. Two-factor ANOVAs revealed that levels of teacher-reported as well as peer-reported relational aggression were significantly lower at time 2 than at time 1 for both intervention groups, and no meaningful change was revealed for the control group. For the long-term intervention group, the lower levels were sustained until time 3. For the short intervention group, we found a significant increase from time 2 to time 3 with regard to teacher reports, even though no significant change emerged from time 2 to time 3 in peer reports.

These results indicate a decrease of bullying behavior in the intervention groups with an effect size of practical value. The frequency of self-reported bullying behavior significantly declined in both intervention groups. The number of bullies and victims decreased or remained constant within the intervention groups but increased in the control group over time, with a significant effect for victimization. We assume an immediate effect of the program, which persists a year after program implementation, because we found a decrease in relational aggression between time 1 and time 2 but no significant change beyond that in the long-term intervention group. Both intervention groups received the program under the same conditions with the exception of the differing number of training sessions over time. This difference in amount of training sessions may explain the unexpected increase in relational aggression in the short-term intervention group at time 3. We assume that the short implementation time of ten weeks is not sufficient to achieve a long-term effect on such a covert behavior as relational aggression.

### Additional analyses study III

On the basis of the Participant Role Questionnaire (PRQ), an instrument based on peer nominations that assigns different social roles to adolescents in the bullying process, we were able to consider another source of information with regard to bullying status besides the self-reports assessed with the BVQ.[16] Three of the participant roles—bullies, assistants, and reinforcers—can be aggregated to form a group of probully actors. After we pooled these groups in our sample at pretest, a group of probullying actors, consisting of forty-one adolescents (twenty-six intervention and fifteen control) resulted. Subsequently, we formed a group of thirty-seven (twenty-seven intervention; ten control) adolescents we called "noninvolved," who were either "outsiders" according to the PRQ or were unclassifiable. We computed a $2 \times 2$ ANOVA for repeated measurement with group (intervention versus control) as the between-factor and time (pre- versus post-) as the within-factor. Analyses revealed no intervention effects for the noninvolved group (see Table 5.2). For the probully group, we did not find any significant effect with self-ratings, but teacher and peer ratings with regard to relational aggression and probully status revealed positive effects for the intervention group: teachers and peers rated probullies' relational aggression higher at pre- than at posttest compared to the control group.[17] In addition, these adolescents received fewer nominations for probullying actions at post than at pretest compared to the control group. Thus, results from self-reports on bullying using the BVQ could be replicated using additional methods (PRQ) and information sources (teacher and peer ratings).

### Conclusion

Meta-analyses revealed that antibullying programs produce small, positive, and statistically significant, but not practically relevant effects, even though they have some meaningful positive effects on

Table 5.2.  Intervention effects for bullying and relational aggression according to bullying role status

| Group | Variable | Intervention | | | | Control | | | | Time × Group Interaction | | |
|---|---|---|---|---|---|---|---|---|---|---|---|---|
| | | Pretest | | Posttest | | Pretest | | Posttest | | | | |
| | | $M$ | SD | $M$ | SD | $M$ | SD | $M$ | SD | $F$ | $p$ | $Eta^2$ |
| Pro-bully-pre | Bully (self) | 1.24 | 0.30 | 1.09 | 0.43 | 1.29 | 0.22 | 1.30 | 0.73 | 1.40 | .24 | .04 |
| | Victim (self) | 1.21 | 0.40 | 1.11 | 0.19 | 1.09 | 0.29 | 1.28 | 0.84 | 3.30 | .08+ | .08 |
| | Relational aggression (self) | 1.61 | 0.68 | 1.50 | 0.47 | 1.50 | 0.73 | 1.41 | 0.47 | 0.00 | .95 | .00 |
| | Relational aggression (teacher) | 2.26 | 1.02 | 1.84 | 0.89 | 1.97 | 0.96 | 1.95 | 0.93 | 4.28 | .04* | .10 |
| | Relational aggression (peer) | 2.29 | 0.61 | 1.90 | 0.71 | 2.33 | 0.56 | 2.56 | 0.83 | 11.01 | .00** | .29 |
| | Pro-bully (peer) | 0.13 | 0.09 | 0.10 | 0.07 | 0.10 | 0.10 | 0.13 | 0.11 | 6.42 | .01* | .14 |
| Uninvolved-pre | Bully (self) | 1.15 | 0.29 | 1.05 | 0.10 | 1.19 | 0.21 | 1.14 | 0.16 | 0.44 | .51 | .03 |
| | Victim (self) | 1.14 | 0.28 | 1.13 | 0.28 | 1.24 | 0.37 | 1.24 | 0.37 | 0.00 | .96 | .00 |
| | Relational aggression (self) | 1.44 | 0.47 | 1.44 | 0.47 | 1.29 | 0.52 | 1.56 | 0.40 | 0.57 | .45 | .02 |
| | Relational aggression (teacher) | 1.67 | 0.69 | 1.34 | 0.51 | 1.78 | 0.70 | 1.76 | 0.81 | 2.42 | .13 | .07 |
| | Relational aggression (peer) | — | | — | | — | | — | | — | | — |
| | Pro-bully (peer) | 0.02 | 0.03 | 0.02 | 0.02 | 0.01 | 0.01 | 0.02 | 0.03 | 3.45 | .07+ | .07 |

*Note:* Pro-bully: $n = 41$ (26 intervention, 15 control); uninvolved: $n = 37$ (27 intervention; 10 control). Analysis for relational aggression in the uninvolved group was not run due to low sample sizes.
+ $p < .10$. * $p < .05$. ** $p < .01$.

bullying behavior.[18,19] In addition, Ryan and Smith report a great variety in outcomes of bullying prevention programs and shortcomings in their evaluation, such as the use of only one type of informant or outcome measure, which decreases the confidence in findings because it only partially depicts bully and victim problems.[20] Finally, although many school-based antibullying programs have been developed and implemented in Europe, there is still a lack of appropriate preventive interventions for relational aggression.[21]

In Germany, no extended programs are promoted and supported by the government so far. Although there is still a lack of research-based, effective, and scientifically evaluated prevention and intervention programs of bullying in Germany, there are localized programs that have shown promising effects (in controlled studies), for example, the adaptation of the Anti-Bullying Programme of Dan Olweus[22] and the program ProACT+ by Spröber and colleagues.[23]

Against this background, the findings reported here show evidence of the effectiveness of the fairplayer.manual in reducing and preventing bullying and relational aggression, as was revealed through pre-post and quasi-experimental studies, with effect sizes of practical value. A positive impact of the intervention program was found on several outcome variables (for example, frequencies of bullies and victims; observed and experienced bullying, relational aggression, prosocial behavior, legitimation of violence, with differences according to treatment integrity).

## *Further development of the program and additional information*

The fairplayer.manual is embedded in publicity strategies and other measures of the nonprofit, registered organization "fairplayer e.V." (www.fairplayer.de). A book with CD-ROM contains all materials (for example, photos, materials for role plays, worksheets, and film materials) and is available on the book market.[24]

For the work in schools, we provide information about bullying, cyberbullying, the legal background, and possibilities for intervening in schools (supported by the "Unfallkasse der Freien Hansestadt Bremen"—all of the pupils in Germany are insured via the statutory accident insurance of the respective federal state).[25] Furthermore, we developed and evaluated a compatible preventive intervention, fairplayer.sport, for sports clubs, also to be implemented as an extracurricular activity.[26] A short film, available in English at youtube.com (http://www.youtube.com/watch? v=64Be5hBmL18), gives an overview of the work with fairplayer. manual and fairplayer.sport.

In the future, we plan to implement the program fairplayer. manual in several of the sixteen German federal states. To accomplish this aim, a train-the-trainer approach will be implemented that will have a multiplier effect in reaching schools. This will be accomplished with financial support from the Deutsche Bahn AG, one of the world's leading passenger and logistics companies, in cooperation with Deutsches Forum für Kriminalprävention, a private law foundation that acts as a national body for crime prevention in Germany by promoting the various approaches that can be undertaken in order to reduce crime, and the Freie Universität Berlin.

To ensure program sustainability, cooperation is planned with the Deutsche Gesellschaft für Demokratiepädagogik e.V. (www.degede.de), an organization promoting education for democratic citizenship characterized by a set of practices and activities designed to help students play an active part in democratic life and exercise their rights and responsibilities in society. Specifically, fairplayer.manual will be implemented with another program, called Class Council.

## Notes

1. Olweus, D. (1994). Annotation: Bullying at school: Basic facts and effects of a school based intervention program. *Journal of Child Psychology and Psychiatry, 35*, 1171–1190.

2. Crick, N. R., & Grotpeter, J. K. (1995). Relational aggression, gender, and social-psychological adjustment. *Child Development, 66*, 710–722.

3. Scheithauer, H., Haag, N., Mahlke, J., & Ittel, A. (2008). Gender-differences in the development of relational aggression: Evidence for an age effect? Preliminary results of a meta-analysis. *European Journal of Developmental Science*, 2, 176–189.

4. Scheithauer, H., Hayer, T., Petermann, F., & Jugert, G. (2006). Physical, verbal and relational forms of bullying among students from Germany: Gender-, age-differences and correlates. *Aggressive Behavior*, 32, 261–275.

5. Schultze-Krumbholz, A., & Scheithauer, H. (2009). Social-behavioural correlates of cyberbullying in a German student sample. *Journal of Psychology*, 217, 224–226.

6. Scheithauer, H., Hayer, T., & Petermann, F. (2003). *Bullying unter Schülern—Erscheinungsformen, Risikobedingungen und Interventionskonzepte*. Göttingen: Hogrefe.

7. Salmivalli, C. (1999). Participant role approach to school bullying: Implications for interventions. *Journal of Adolescence*, 22, 453–459.

8. Salmivalli, C. (2010). Bullying and the peer group: A review. *Aggression and Violent Behavior*, 15, 112–120.

9. Smith, P. K. (2004). Bullying: Recent developments. *Child and Adolescent Mental Health*, 9, 98–103.

10. Stassen Berger, K. (2007). Update on bullying at school: Science forgotten? *Developmental Review*, 27, 90–126.

11. Scheithauer, H., & Bull, H. D. (2008). *fairplayer.manual: Förderung von sozialen Kompetenzen und Zivilcourage—Prävention von Bullying und Schulgewalt*. Göttingen: Vandenhoeck & Ruprecht.

12. Malti, T., Häcker, T., & Nakamura, Y. (2009). *Kluge Gefühle? Sozial-emotionales Lernen in der Schule*. Zürich: Verlag Psetalozzianum.

13. Scheithauer, H., & Bull, H. D. (2007). Unterrichtsbegleitende Förderung sozialer Kompetenzen und Prävention von Bullying im Jugendalter—das fairplayer.manual. *Gruppenpsychotherapie und Gruppendynamik*, 43, 277–293.

14. Scheithauer, H., & Bull, H. D. (2010). Das fairplayer.manual zur unterrichtsbegleitenden Förderung sozialer Kompetenzen und Prävention von Bullying im Jugendalter: Ergebnisse der Pilotevaluation. *Praxis der Kinderpsychologie und Kinderpsychiatrie*, 59, 266–281.

15. Bull, H., Schultze, M., & Scheithauer, H. (2009). School-based prevention of bullying and relational aggression: The fairplayer.manual. *European Journal of Developmental Science*, 3, 312–317.

16. Salmivalli, C., Lagerspetz, K., Björkqvist, K., Österman, K., & Kaukiainen, A. (1996). Bullying as a group process: Participant roles and their relations to social status within the group. *Aggressive Behavior*, 22, 1–15.

17. Kärnä, A., Voeten, M., Little, T. D., Poskiparta, E., Kaljonen, A., & Salmivalli, C. (2011). A large-scale evaluation of the KiVa Antibullying Program: Grades 4–6. *Child Development*, 82, 311–330.

18. Ferguson, C. J., Miguel, C. S., Kilburn, J. C., & Sanchez, P. (2007). The effectiveness of school based anti-bullying programs: A meta-analytic review. *Criminal Justice Review*, 32, 401–414.

19. Merrell, K. W., Gueldner, B. A., Ross, S. W., & Isava, D. M. (2008). How effective are school bullying intervention programs? A meta-analysis of intervention research. *School Psychology Quarterly, 23*, 26–42.

20. Ryan, W., & Smith, J. D. (2009). Antibullying programs in schools: How effective are evaluation practices? *Prevention Science.* doi:10.1007/s11121-009-0128-y.

21. Ostrov, J. M., Massetti, G. M., Stauffacher, K., Godleski, S. A., Hart, K. C., Karch, K. M., Mullins, I.D., & Ries, E. E. (2008). An intervention for relational and physical aggression in early childhood: A preliminary study. *Early Childhood Research Quarterly, 36*, 311–322.

22. Hanewinkel, R. (2004). Prevention of bullying in German schools: An evaluation of an anti-bullying approach. In P. K. Smith, D. Pepler, & K. Rigby (Eds.), *Bullying in schools. How successful can interventions be?* (pp. 81–98). Cambridge: Cambridge University Press.

23. Spröber, N., Schlottke, P. F., & Hautzinger, M. (2006). ProACT + E: Ein Programm zur Prävention von "bullying" an Schulen und zur Förderung der positiven Entwicklung von Schülern. *Zeitschrift für Klinische Psychologie und Psychotherapie, 35*, 140–150.

24. Scheithauer, H., & Bull, H. D. (2008). *fairplayer.manual: Förderung von sozialen Kompetenzen und Zivilcourage—Prävention von Bullying und Schulgewalt.* Göttingen: Vandenhoeck & Ruprecht.

25. Schultze-Krumbholz, A., Scheithauer, H., & Braun, D. (2009). *Zum Umgang mit Bullying und Cyberbullying in der Schule: Eine Handreichung für Lehrerinnen und Lehrer im Bundesland Bremen.* Bremen: Unfallkasse Freie Hansestadt Bremen. http://www.unfallkasse.bremen.de /pdf-dl.php?id=18&type=1.

26. Scheithauer, H., Hess, M., Haag, N., & Pawlizki, C. (2010). Ausbildung zur sozialen Kompetenz: Konzeption und Evaluation des Programms fairplayer.sport. In O. Höner, R. Schreiner, & F. Schultz (Hrsg.), *Aus- und Fortbildungskonzepte im Fußball—Beiträge und Analysen zum Fußballsport XVII. Tagungsband in der dvs-Schriftenreihe, Band 206* (pp. 54–68). Hamburg: Czwalina; Scheithauer, H., Hess, M., & Pawlizki, C. (2010). fairplayer.sport–ein bewegungsorientiertes Programm zur Förderung moralischer, sozialer und emotionaler Kompetenzen. In B. Latzko & T. Malti (Eds.), *Moralische Entwicklung und Erziehung in Kindheit und Adoleszenz* (pp. 221–240). Göttingen: Hogrefe.

HERBERT SCHEITHAUER *is a professor of developmental psychology and clinical psychology and head of the Division of Developmental Science and Applied Developmental Psychology at Freie Universität Berlin.*

MARKUS HESS *is a scientific staff member at the Division of Developmental Science and Applied Developmental Psychology at Freie Universität Berlin.*

ANJA SCHULTZE-KRUMBHOLZ *is a doctoral candidate and scientific staff member at the Division of Developmental Science and Applied Developmental Psychology at Freie Universität Berlin.*

HEIKE DELE BULL *is a doctoral candidate at the Division of Developmental Science and Applied Developmental Psychology at Freie Universität Berlin.*

*Consistent and cooperative actions are key elements for effective bullying prevention and intervention. The ViSC Social Competence Program fosters a school development process and offers training to work against violence.*

# 6

## ViSC Social Competence Program

*Dagmar Strohmeier, Christine Hoffmann, Eva-Maria Schiller, Elisabeth Stefanek, Christiane Spiel*

THE IMPLEMENTATION AND evaluation of the ViSC Social Competence Program was funded between 2008 and 2011 by the Austrian federal Ministry for Education.

Research activities on the topic of violence prevention in Austrian schools were initiated in the mid-1990s.[1] In 2003, a national report summarizing existing initiatives to prevent violence and bullying in Austrian schools showed that they were neither evidence based nor successful.[2] Several initiatives had been undertaken by teachers in Austrian schools, but they did not meet scientific quality standards, and as a result, these uncoordinated efforts were highly ineffective.

At the beginning of 2007, as a result of a quick succession of several spectacular events in schools and the ensuing public discussion on the high rates of bullying among Austrian youth, the Austrian Federal Ministry for Education commissioned researchers to develop a national strategy for violence prevention in the Austrian public school system.[3] The goal was to develop a procedure that had the following components: (a) making bullying prevention a

NEW DIRECTIONS FOR YOUTH DEVELOPMENT, NO. 133, SPRING 2012 © WILEY PERIODICALS, INC.
Published online in Wiley Online Library (wileyonlinelibrary.com) • DOI: 10.1002/yd.20008

common goal of as many stakeholder groups as possible in Austria, (b) learning from research and international examples, and (c) applying evidence-based programs in Austrian schools.

The national strategy, Together Against Violence, covered six activity domains:

1. Policy and advocacy
2. Information and public relations
3. Networking and cooperation
4. Knowledge transfer and education
5. Prevention and intervention
6. Evaluation and research

In 2008, the national strategy became part of the coalition agreement between the two governing parties and has been extended and financially supported until 2013. Examples of activities within the national strategy were the development of a national home page, the organization of annual conferences for stakeholder groups, the development of an online self-evaluation tool for schools, and the implementation and evaluation of the ViSC program.[4]

---

### Goals and target groups of the ViSC program

In accordance with the Austrian national strategy, the main goal of the ViSC program is to reduce aggressive behavior and bullying and foster social and intercultural competencies in schools. The ViSC program is a primary preventive program designed for secondary schools. In Austria, secondary schools serve grades 5 to 8, with students aged eleven to fifteen years. The ViSC program intends to install the mission of the national strategy, Together Against Violence, as a commonly shared principle in schools, approaches the school as a whole, and uses a systemic perspective. The prevention of aggression and bullying is defined as a school development task, and the initial implementation of the program lasts one school year. During the first semester, the program covers interventive and preventive measures at the school, and teachers are the primary target group (see Table 6.1). Preventive measures at the class level are introduced to the teachers during the second semester. During this semester, the target groups are both teachers and students.

## Bridging research and practice

To foster sustainable knowledge transfer between research and practice, a cascaded train-the-trainer model has been developed and applied: scientists train ViSC coaches (who are called multipliers), multipliers train teachers, and teachers train their students.

A ViSC course for training multipliers was offered at the University of Vienna for three consecutive years. Each course consisted of three face-to-face workshops held at the University of Vienna within one academic year (between September and June) and the simultaneous implementation of the ViSC program in one school during the same time span (for details, see Table 6.1). The ViSC coaches were recruited by the Austrian Federal Ministry of Education through official invitation letters that were sent to all rectors (top administrators) of the teaching universities and the heads of the school psychology services in Austria. The idea was to train permanent staff working at the teaching universities or in the school psychology services to enable sustainable knowledge transfer between research and practice.

The ViSC courses aimed at providing ViSC coaches with state-of-the art knowledge about bullying research, introducing them to the philosophy and the tools of the ViSC program, and offering them detailed instructions on how best to implement the ViSC program in schools. The implementation in schools consisted of three informative meetings during pedagogical conferences: two in-school training sessions and several individual or small group coaching sessions (for details, see Table 6.1). All materials necessary for these training sessions (for example, worksheets and guidelines) were provided to the ViSC coaches during the ViSC course and by an online-learning platform. There was no cost to attending the ViSC course at the University of Vienna, and the

## Table 6.1. The ViSC course for ViSC coaches

| Month | Activity | Content |
|---|---|---|
| September | Two-day workshop at the University of Vienna | State-of-the-art knowledge about bullying research<br>Knowledge about standards of evidence<br>Overview of the ViSC program<br>Detailed instructions on how to implement the program at the school level |
| September | First pedagogical conference in the school | General information about the program to all teachers |
| September–October | In-school training | Definition and recognition of the problem<br>Tackling acute cases<br>How best to implement preventive measures at the school level |
| October–February | Coaching of the school team | How to engage as many people as possible in the school<br>How to involve parents |
| February | Second pedagogical conference in the school | Reflection about the implementation process at school level and how best to continue the activities |
| February | Two-day workshop at the University of Vienna | Reflection on the implementation processes in the schools and the professional role of ViSC coaches<br>Detailed instructions on how to implement the program at the class level<br>Continuation of implementation at the school level |
| February–March | In-school training | Preventive measures at the class level: Content and implementation of the class project |
| March–June | Class and school team coaching | How to continue activities at the school level<br>How best to implement the units of the class project |
| June | One-day workshop at the University of Vienna | Reflection on the implementation processes in the schools and the professional role as a ViSC coach |
| June | Third pedagogical conference in the school | Reflection on implementation of the program and how best to continue the activities in the next school year without the ViSC coach |

NEW DIRECTIONS FOR YOUTH DEVELOPMENT • DOI: 10.1002/yd

ViSC coaches received the standard salary usually paid by teaching universities for in-school teacher training.

## The implementation process in the schools

The main goal during the program implementation is to create a school development process during which as many teachers as possible are committed to work together against violence. The ViSC program aims to foster shared responsibility among teachers, which in turn implies that as many teachers as possible in the school have worked out a common understanding of the problem, agreed on procedures for tackling acute cases, and jointly implement preventive measures at the school and class levels. The theory behind this approach is that bullying is promoted in an environment in which the problem is not taken seriously or is overlooked and that bullying can be stopped in an environment in which there is a consensus that such behavior will not be tolerated.

The ViSC coach has a central role during this process. This person is an expert who provides state-of-the-art knowledge and introduces specific procedures for how best to tackle the problem and implement preventive measures at the school and class levels. This person is also a coach who must be able to integrate the existing expertise of the teachers in order to commit and empower as many of them as possible. The ability of the ViSC coach to foster ownership of the program by the school staff is considered central to a sustainable school development process. Besides the implementation of this philosophy of the program, the ViSC coach also offers many practical tools during the in-school training for the teachers.

## The teacher training

Two in-school teacher trainings are offered (see Table 6.1). During the first session, which is offered at the beginning of the first semester, teachers are trained on how to recognize bullying, how to tackle acute bullying cases, and how to implement preventive measures at the school level. In accordance with the philosophy of the program, the training contains many interactive elements to foster the development of a commonly shared perspective among as many teachers as possible.

In accordance with the training goals, the first in-school training is divided into three parts.

### Definition and recognition of the problem

To provide an overview of the understanding of violence, aggression, and bullying versus teachers' social and intercultural competence, the ViSC coach prompts a brainstorming discussion. The goal is to collect ideas without judging them as right or wrong. During the discussion, it becomes clear whether there are contradictory opinions among the teachers and whether and to what extent teachers have already worked on these issues. Next, the coach introduces the scientific perspective by discussing the broad definition of violence from the World Health Organization and the much narrower definition of bullying.[5] The scientific definitions of social competence are also discussed.[6] By acknowledging the previous knowledge of the teachers, the ViSC coach leads them to the insight that it is very helpful for prevention and intervention to have a common understanding of the problem and that bullying is a serious issue that needs to be tackled.

The teachers next work in small groups and analyze hypothetical cases. The goal is to discuss how to detect bullying and how to differentiate it from reactive aggression, rejection, shyness, or voluntary solitude. These discussions usually reveal that it is not always easy to detect bullying and that it is very helpful that teachers work together to get the information needed.

### Tackling acute bullying cases

It is very important for both intervention and prevention that the teachers follow a common procedure in addressing acute bullying cases. Based on the work of Roland and Vaaland and in line with their suggestions, a best practice procedure is introduced to the teachers.[7] To tackle a bullying case, the teachers need to talk with the victimized student first. Second, they need to talk with the bullying students by clearly stating that this behavior is wrong and needs to be stopped immediately. These conversations need to be firm but respectful. If a group of students has bullied another student, the conversations need to be conducted in such a way as to weaken the social bonds of the bullying students. Third, it is necessary to inform the parents. The teachers are provided with a detailed manual including examples of sentences for how to conduct these conversations. Extending the work from Roland and Vaaland, the manual also covers example conversations with students who both bully others and are victimized by others and their parents.

### Preventive measures on the school level

Even before participating in the ViSC program, many schools have already implemented some preventive measures. The ViSC coach aims to integrate these existing measures in a common schoolwide approach to prevent violence. For instance, some schools have already implemented peer education approaches that are suitable complementary methods to the ViSC program. Some teachers are experts in peer mediation techniques; these are not suitable for tackling bullying cases, but they can be integrated in a schoolwide approach to solving conflicts between parties of equal strength.

The task of the ViSC coach is to clarify which method is suitable for which goals. The coach aims to commit teachers to tackling acute bullying cases according to the guidelines presented in the manual and works on an agreement that clarifies who will be responsible for conducting these conversations. The teachers who are willing to coordinate the activities at the school level are nominated to be part of the school team. These teachers also prepare information sheets about the ViSC program for students and parents. Finally, the ViSC coach works on an agreement as to how best to implement a ViSC class project during the second semester. It needs to be clarified which classes will participate in the class project, which teachers will implement it, and how the teaching units needed for the class project can best be integrated in the curriculum of these classes.

The second in-school teacher training is offered at the beginning of the second semester. Its main goal is to introduce the philosophy and materials of the ViSC class project to all teachers to enable them to implement it in their classes. This training also contains many interactive elements like role plays and interactive games because it is intended that teachers apply some of these methods in their classes when they implement the class project.

## The class project

The class project aims to empower students to take responsibility for what happens in their class. The project is divided into two parts. During units 1 to 8, the students work together to find ways to prevent aggressive behavior in their class. During units 9 to 13, the students work together to achieve a positive, common goal (for details see Table 6.2).

Thus, the class project is not an antibullying program in a narrow sense. Instead, the goal is to train a broad spectrum of competencies considered important for the development of social and intercultural competencies (see also Table 6.2). The idea behind this approach is that different students need to learn different competencies. In many classes, a rather large group of students neither feels responsible for what happens around them nor intervenes in critical situations.[8] Therefore, all students are trained to feel responsible when something negative is going on and to react in a way that is likely to improve the situation. Second, in lower secondary school, there is still a group of preadolescents who are not able to manage their negative emotions in a nonaggressive way.[9] Therefore, all students are trained to recognize their own emotions and the emotions of others and to cope with these emotions in a positive, nonaggressive way. Third, it is necessary to empower students who might be victimized easily because they often invite attacks with their nonassertive behavior.[10] Thus, all students are trained how best to react when others are picking on them. The class project does not include units to directly change

## Table 6.2. The ViSC class project

| Unit | Content |
| --- | --- |
| Unit 1 | What is the class project, and why are we participating? Why are rules important in our lives, and what rules do we want in our class? |
| Unit 2 | How can we recognize critical social situations, and what can we do to help improve the situation? |
| Unit 3 | How can we recognize the emotions of others, and what can we do to help them feel better? |
| Unit 4 | How can we recognize our own emotions, and what can we do to cope with them to feel better? |
| Units 5–6 | What can we do if we are treated in a mean and unfair way by others? What is the best thing to do in such situations, and why? |
| Units 7–8 | What can we do if we don't understand the behavior of our classmates who come from another country? What is the best thing to do in such situations, and why? |
| Unit 9 | What have we learned during the project so far, and what do we want to learn in the remaining units? Which common activity do we want to carry out during our project day? How can we plan and organize the common activity in a way that every classmate is able to make a valuable contribution? |
| Units 10–13 | Carrying out the common activity by creating a process that leads to the experience of a common success. |

the behavior of bullying students; instead the class project aims to create an environment in which it is less likely that bullying will occur.

To train these competencies, concrete materials are provided in the manual. Each unit is designed for a two-hour lesson and consists of worksheets for individual students, sheets for small group work, summary sheets, and a detailed implementation plan. The task of the teacher is to lead the class and work with the materials provided in the manual. The units are designed to foster exchange and discussions among the students. The teacher is encouraged to use interactive games, role plays, and other interactive pedagogical methods that were demonstrated to them during the second in-school teacher training and explained in the manual.

During unit 9, the focus of the class project changes. Whereas the students worked on hypothetical situations and prepared materials during units 1 to 8, now they take responsibility for the remaining units. To transfer the social competencies into real life, the class is assigned to find a common, positive, and realistic activity that can be carried out together during a project day. The role of the teacher is to create a group process that enables cooperative learning and the experience of a common success. Thus, the teacher helps the students find a cooperative structure and supervises them as they plan and carry out the activity. A huge variety of activities has been carried out during ViSC project days. Some classes produced photos, short films, songs, or newspapers. Others conducted interviews with students in other classes, people on the street, and local politicians and asked them about their contribution to preventing violence. Still others organized parents' meetings during which they wrote a performance to demonstrate what they had learned during the class project.

To summarize, the theoretical idea is that aggressive behavior is less likely to occur in an encouraging, structured, and friendly environment where students are able to feel part of a group and are able to create common successes.

## Evaluation studies of the class project

In a pilot phase, the ViSC class project has been implemented four times, and program evaluations have confirmed encouraging short-term results.[11] However, the evaluations also demonstrated that the class project was not effective to prevent aggressive behavior in the long run. Therefore, the evaluation results were used to improve the structure and materials of the ViSC class project and to develop the final ViSC program, which also covers teacher training, measures at the school level, and actions to take.

## Large-scale evaluation of the ViSC school program

Between May 2009 and December 2010, a large-scale evaluation study was conducted. It was possible to realize a randomized intervention-control group design and to collect data from 2,042 students on four occasions.[12] Furthermore, 338 teachers participated in a survey at pretest and posttest.[13]

Yanagida and colleagues investigated the short-term effectiveness (pre- and post test) of the program with respect to aggressive behavior and victimization.[14] For this study, three self-report scales to measure aggressive behavior and three self-report scales to measure victimization were used. A multiple group latent change score (LCS) model to compare the control and intervention group was applied.[15] Gender and age were included as covariates to control for baseline and intervention effects. The multiple group LCS model imposing strict measurement invariance fit the data well: $\chi^2$ (181) = 544.065, $p$ < 0.01, CFI = .922, RMSEA = .044. Results showed that the latent mean of the aggression change score in the intervention group differed significantly from 0 ($M = -0.23$, $p = $ .013), indicating a decline in aggressive behavior. For victimization, however, the latent mean of the change factor was not significantly different from 0 ($M = -0.16$, $p = $ .108). Age did not have any effects on aggression and victimization; boys scored higher in aggression at time 1 and had a lower decrease over time. In accordance with the main goals of the ViSC program, aggression could be reduced in participating students.

Burger and colleagues investigated whether teachers used different strategies to tackle bullying cases before and after the program.[16] Data was collected using the Handling Bullying Questionnaire (HBQ) to evaluate the effectiveness of the program regarding the strategy use of teachers.[17] Results showed that teachers who participated in the program used more nonpunitive strategies to work with the bullies and more strategies to support victims compared with teachers who did not participate in the program.[18]

However, investigating goal attainment is only the first step in the research program. Future studies will investigate the theoretical model and underlying mechanisms of the intervention effects in depth. Furthermore, subgroups of students (such as onlookers, bullies, victims, and bully-victims) will be the focus of further analyses. Because follow-up data were collected, additional longitudinal analyses will be conducted.

## Notes

1. Singer, M., & Spiel, C. (1998). Erprobung eines Anti-Aggressionsprogramms an österreichischen Schulen—Erste Ergebnisse [Establishing a program against violence in Austrian schools: First results]. In J. Glück, O. Vitouch, M. Jirasko, & B. Rollett (Eds.), *Perspektiven psychologischer Forschung in Österreich* (Vol. 2, pp. 223–226). Vienna, Austria: WUV; Robier, C., & Spiel, C. (1998). Aggressionsbekämpfung in Hauptschulen: Zum Einfluss von Angst und Gewalt im Fernsehen [Tackling aggression in general secondary schools: The influence of anxiety and violence on TV]. In J. Glück, O. Vitouch, M. Jirasko, & B. Rollett (Eds.), *Perspektiven psychologischer Forschung in Österreich* (Vol. 2, pp. 227–230). Vienna, Austria: WUV.

2. Atria, M., & Spiel, C. (2003). The Austrian situation: Many initiatives against violence, few evaluations. In P. K. Smith (Ed.), *Violence in schools: The response in Europe* (pp. 83–99). London: Routledge Falmer.

3. Craig, W., & Harel, Y. (2004). Bullying, physical fighting and victimization. In C. Currie (Ed.), *Health behaviour in school-aged children: A WHO cross national study* (pp. 133–144). Geneva: World Health Organization; Currie, C., Roberts, C., Morgan, A., Smith, R., Settertobulte, W., Samdal, O., & Barnekow, V. (2004). *Young people's health in context. Health Behaviour in School-Aged Children (HBSC) study: International report from the 2001/2002 survey.* Geneva: World Health Organization; Spiel, C. & Strohmeier, D. (2012). Evidence-based practice and policy: When researchers, policy makers, and practitioners learn how to work together. *European Journal of Developmental Psychology, 9,* 150–162; Spiel, C., & Strohmeier, D. (2011). National strategy for violence prevention in the Austrian public school system: Development and implementation. *International Journal of Behavioral Development, 35,* 412–418; Spiel, C., & Strohmeier, D. (2007). *Generalstrategie zur Gewaltprävention an österreichischen Schulen und Kindergärten "Gemeinsam gegen Gewalt"* [General strategy for violence prevention in Austrian schools and kindergartens "Together against violence"]. Report to the Federal Ministry of Education, Arts, and Cultural Affairs. Vienna, Austria: University of Vienna.

4. Spiel, C., Strohmeier, D., Schultes, M. T., & Burger, C. (2011). *Nachhaltigkeit von Gewaltprävention in Schulen: Erstellung und Erprobung eines Selbstevaluationsinstruments* [Sustainable violence prevention in schools: Development and evaluation of a self evaluation tool for schools]. Report to the Federal Ministry of Education, Arts, and Cultural Affairs. Vienna, Austria: University of Vienna; Atria, M., & Spiel, C. (2007). The Viennese Social Competence (ViSC) training for students: Program and evaluation. In J. E. Zins, M. J. Elias, & C. A. Maher (Eds.), *Bullying, victimization and peer harassment: A handbook of prevention and intervention* (pp. 179–198). New York, NY: Haworth Press; Strohmeier, D., Atria, M., & Spiel, C. (2008). WiSK: Ein ganzheitliches Schulprogramm zur Förderung sozialer Kompetenz und Prävention aggressiven Verhaltens [ViSC: A whole school policy program to promote social competence and prevent aggressive behavior]. In T. Malti & S. Perren (Eds.), *Soziale Kompetenzen bei Kindern und Jugendlichen* (pp. 214–230). Stuttgart: Kohlhammer.

5. Krug, E. G., Dahlberg, L. L., Mercy, J. A., Zwi, A. B., & Lozano, R. (2002). *World report on violence and health.* Geneva: World Health Organization; Olweus, D. (1978). *Aggression in the schools: Bullies and whipping boys.* Washington, DC: Hemisphere Press; Olweus, D. (1993). *Bullying at school: What we know and what we can do.* Oxford: Blackwell; Roland, E. (1989). A system oriented strategy against bullying. In E. Roland & E. Munthe (Eds.), *Bullying: An international perspective.* London: David Fulton.

6. Rose-Krasnor, L. (1997). The nature of social competence: A theoretical review. *Social Development, 6,* 111–135; Rubin, K. H., & Rose-Krasnor, L. (1992). Interpersonal problem solving. In V. B. Van Hasset & M. Hersen (Eds.), *Handbook of social development* (pp. 283–323). New York, NY: Plenum.

7. Roland, E., & Vaaland, G. (2006). *ZERO teacher's guide to the Zero Anti-Bullying Programme.* Stavanger: Centre for Behavioural Research, University of Stavanger.

8. Craig, W., Pepler, D., & Atlas, R. (2000). Observations of bullying in the playground and in the classroom. *School Psychology International, 21,* 22–36; O'Connel, P., Pepler, D., & Craig, W. M. (1999). Peer involvement in bullying: Insights and challenges for intervention. *Journal of Adolescence, 22,* 437–452.

9. Roland, E., & Idsøe, T. (2001). Aggression and bullying. *Aggressive Behavior, 27,* 446–462; Salmivalli, C., & Nieminen, E. (2002). Proactive and reactive aggression among school bullies, victims, and bully-victims. *Aggressive Behavior, 28,* 30–44.

10. Veenstra, R., Lindenberg, S., Zijlstra, B.J.H., De Winter, A. F., Verhulst, F. C., & Ormel, J. (2007). The dyadic nature of bullying and victimization: Testing a dual-perspective theory. *Child Development, 78*(6), 1843–1854.

11. Atria, M., & Spiel, C. (2007). The Viennese Social Competence (ViSC) training for students: Program and evaluation. In J. E. Zins, M. J. Elias, & C. A. Maher (Eds.), *Bullying, victimization and peer harassment: A handbook of prevention and intervention* (pp. 179–198). New York: The Haworth Press; Gollwitzer, M. (2005). Könnten Anti-Aggressions-Trainings in der Schule wirksamer sein, wenn sie weniger standardisiert wären? In A. Ittel & M. v Salisch (Eds.), *Lästern, Lügen, Leiden lassen: Aggressives Verhalten von Kindern und Jugendlichen* (pp. 276–312). Stuttgart: Kohlhammer; Gollwitzer, M., Banse, R., Eisenbach, K., & Naumann, E. (2007). Effectiveness of the Vienna social competence training on implicit and explicit aggression. Evidence from an Aggressiveness IAT. *European Journal of Psychological Assessment, 23,* 150–156; Gollwitzer, M., Eisenbach, K., Atria, M., Strohmeier, D., & Banse, R. (2006). Evaluation of aggression-reducing effects of the "Viennese Social Competence Training." *Swiss Journal of Psychology, 65*(2), 125–135.

12. Spiel, C., Strohmeier, D., Schiller, E. M., Stefanek, E., Schultes, M. T., Hoffmann, C., Yanagida, T., . . . Pollhammer, B. (2011). WiSK Programm: Förderung sozialer und interkultureller Kompetenzen in der Schule. WiSK Evaluationsstudie: Abschlussbericht [ViSC social competence program. Evaluation study: Final report]. Report to the Federal Ministry of Education, Arts, and Cultural Affairs. Vienna, Austria: University of Vienna.

13. Burger, C., Strohmeier, D., Stefanek, E., Schiller E. M., & Spiel, C. (2011, July). *Effects of the Viennese Social Competence Training (ViSC) on teachers' strategy use for tackling bullying.* Poster presented at the 12th European Congress of Psychology (ECP), Istanbul, Turkey.

14. Yanagida, T., Schiller E. M., Strohmeier, D., Stefanek, E., von Eye, A., & Spiel, C. (2011, August). *Evaluation of the ViSC Social Competence Program in Austria.* Poster presented at the 15th European Conference on Developmental Psychology (ECDP), Bergen, Norway.

15. McArdle, J. J., & Prindle, J. J. (2008). A latent change score analysis of a randomized clinical trial in reasoning training. *Psychology and Aging, 23,* 702–719.

16. Burger et al. (2011).

17. Bauman, S., Rigby, K., & Hoppa, K. (2008). US teachers' and school councellors' strategies for handling school bullying incidents. *Educational Psychology, 28,* 837–856; Rigby, K., & Bauman, S. (2010). How school personnel tackle cases of bullying: A critical examination. In S. R. Jimerson, S. M. Swearer, & D. L. Espelage (Eds.), *Handbook of bullying in schools: An international perspective* (pp. 455–467). New York, NY: Routledge/Taylor & Francis Group; Strohmeier, D., Sproeber, N., Burger, C., Bauman, S., & Rigby, K. *Teachers' strategies for tackling bullying cases in schools in Austria and Germany.*

18. Spiel et al. (2011).

DAGMAR STROHMEIER *is professor at the School of Health/Social Sciences at the University of Applied Sciences Upper Austria, Linz, Austria.*

CHRISTINE HOFFMANN *is a trainer, coach, and member of the ViSC team based at the University of Vienna and the University of Applied Sciences Upper Austria.*

EVA-MARIA SCHILLER *is a research associate at the Institute of Developmental Psychology, University of Muenster, Germany.*

ELISABETH STEFANEK *is a postdoctoral researcher at the University of Applied Sciences Upper Austria, Linz, Austria.*

CHRISTIANE SPIEL *is founding professor for Bildung-Psychology and Evaluation at the University of Vienna and its department head.*

*Systematic and meta-analytic reviews of longitudinal studies demonstrate that antibullying programs could be viewed as a form of early crime prevention as well as an early form of public health promotion.*

# 7

# Risk and protective factors, longitudinal research, and bullying prevention

*Maria M. Ttofi, David P. Farrington*

SCHOOL BULLYING IS a serious problem that affects one in five school-aged children worldwide.[1] Given the serious short-term and long-term effects on children's physical and mental health, it is understandable that school bullying has increasingly become a central topic in intervention and evaluation research.[2] School bullying has recently become a topic of major public concern and has drawn media attention, with articles in major newspapers and magazines reporting cases of children who committed (or attempted) suicide because of their victimization at school and parents suing school authorities for their failure to protect their offspring from continued bullying victimization.[3] But is there scientific evidence about the detrimental effects of school bullying on children's physical and mental health? Or is school bullying merely a part of a developmental process, one of those school experiences said to prepare children for the grown-up world, as some skeptics argue?

NEW DIRECTIONS FOR YOUTH DEVELOPMENT, NO. 133, SPRING 2012 © WILEY PERIODICALS, INC.
Published online in Wiley Online Library (wileyonlinelibrary.com) • DOI: 10.1002/yd.20009

## Adverse outcomes for children involved in school bullying

Bullying continues to be a serious problem plaguing school youth in both developed and developing countries.[4] Scientific interest in the problem of bullying and its negative short-term and long-term effects emerged after the well-publicized suicides of three Norwegian boys in 1982, which were attributed to severe peer bullying.[5] Longitudinal research has been carried out to investigate the long-term negative effects of school bullying. In his follow-up study of over seven hundred Stockholm boys, Olweus reported that 36 percent of bullies at ages thirteen to sixteen were convicted three or more times between ages sixteen and twenty-four, compared with 10 percent of the remainder.[6] Scientific research has also established the intergenerational transmission of school bullying: in the Cambridge Study in Delinquent Development, for example, boys who were bullies at age fourteen tended, at age thirty-two, to have children who were bullies.[7]

There have been surprisingly few recently published longitudinal studies on the developmental pathways of children involved in school bullying since the seminal work of Olweus in Scandinavia. Two special issues in peer-reviewed journals have recently been organized in an attempt to address this gap in research literature.[8] Both issues presented new findings on the long-term negative consequences of school bullying based on major prospective longitudinal studies from around the world. Longitudinal investigators of twenty-nine studies conducted analyses for the aims of a more comprehensive British Academy Funded Project, which examines the long-term association of school bullying with both internalizing (such as anxiety, self-esteem, and stress) and externalizing (such as aggression, alcohol, and drug use) problems.

The special issue of *Criminal Behaviour and Mental Health* focused on the association between bullying perpetration at school and offending later in life. A systematic review and meta-analysis on the topic was carried out.[9] It was found that the probability of offending

## Figure 7.1. Bullying perpetration versus offending: Adjusted effect sizes

| Model | Study name | Statistics for each study | | | | | Odds ratio and 95% CI |
|---|---|---|---|---|---|---|---|
| | | Odds ratio | Lower limit | Upper limit | Z-Value | p-Value | |
| | ENLSB | 8.121 | 2.814 | 23.436 | 3.873 | 0.000 | |
| | MLS | 5.100 | 2.389 | 10.889 | 4.210 | 0.000 | |
| | NFLS | 2.900 | 1.155 | 7.281 | 2.267 | 0.023 | |
| | JLS | 2.732 | 2.177 | 3.428 | 8.679 | 0.000 | |
| | SU12OP | 1.920 | 1.081 | 3.412 | 2.224 | 0.026 | |
| | ESYTC | 1.898 | 1.620 | 2.224 | 7.916 | 0.000 | |
| | ATP | 1.849 | 1.140 | 2.999 | 2.491 | 0.013 | |
| | IYDS | 1.708 | 1.123 | 2.598 | 2.501 | 0.012 | |
| | ENDPS | 1.702 | 1.372 | 2.110 | 4.840 | 0.000 | |
| | PYS | 1.660 | 0.967 | 2.850 | 1.837 | 0.066 | |
| | MACS2 | 1.494 | 0.943 | 2.366 | 1.711 | 0.087 | |
| | CSDD | 1.490 | 0.711 | 3.123 | 1.056 | 0.291 | |
| | MACS1 | 1.440 | 0.845 | 2.453 | 1.342 | 0.180 | |
| | CHDS | 1.409 | 0.883 | 2.249 | 1.438 | 0.151 | |
| | RHCP | 1.388 | 1.102 | 1.749 | 2.780 | 0.005 | |
| Fixed | | 1.861 | 1.707 | 2.028 | 14.102 | 0.000 | |
| Random | | 1.886 | 1.598 | 2.227 | 7.490 | 0.000 | |

0.01    0.1    1    10    100
Favors Nonoffending    Favors Offending

*Note:* ATP = Australian Temperament Project; CHDS = Christchurch Health and Development Study; CSDD = Cambridge Study in Delinquent Development; ENDPS = Erlangen-Nuremberg Development and Prevention Study; ENLSB = Erlangen-Nuremberg Longitudinal Study of Bullying; ESYTC = Edinburgh Study of Youth Transitions and Crime; IYDS = International Youth and Development Study; JLS = Japanese Longitudinal Study; MACS1 = Metropolitan Area Child Study, Cohort 1; MACS2 = Metropolitan Area Child Study, Cohort 2; MLS = Montreal Longitudinal Study; NFLS = Nationwide 1981 Finnish Longitudinal Study; PYS = Pittsburgh Youth Study; RHCP = Raising Health Children Project; SU12OP = Snap Under 12 Outreach Project.

up to 16.5 years later (mean follow-up period: 5.84 years) was much higher for school bullies than for noninvolved students (unadjusted odds ratio [OR] = 2.54; 95 percent CI: 2.05—3.14). Bullying perpetration was a significant risk factor for later offending even after controlling for major childhood risk factors that were measured before school bullying (adjusted OR = 1.89, 95 percent CI: 1.60—2.23); see Figure 7.1. In other words, children who bully at school are about twice as likely as nonbullies to be involved in offending later in life. This important finding suggests that school bullying is a unique and independent childhood risk factor for later offending.

The special issue of the *Journal of Aggression, Conflict and Peace Research* focused on the association between bullying victimization (that is, being bullied) and internalizing problems later in life, such as anxiety and depression. A systematic review and meta-analysis was carried out examining the extent to which bullying victimization at school predicts depression later in life and whether this relation holds after controlling for other major childhood risk factors that were measured before school bullying.[10] The probability of being depressed up to 36 years later (mean follow-up period: 7.13 years) was much higher for children who were bullied at school than for noninvolved students (unadjusted OR = 1.99; 95 percent CI: 1.69–2.33). Bullying victimization was a significant risk factor for later depression even after controlling for up to twenty (mean number of 6.42 covariates) major childhood risk factors (adjusted OR = 1.71; 95 percent CI: 1.49–1.96); see Figure 7.2). In other words, children who are bullied at school are about

**Figure 7.2. Bullying victimization versus depression: Adjusted effect sizes**

| Model | Study name | Odds ratio | Lower limit | Upper limit | Z-Value | p-Value |
|---|---|---|---|---|---|---|
| | AMHC | 3.249 | 1.664 | 6.343 | 3.452 | 0.001 |
| | NFLS | 2.258 | 0.894 | 5.702 | 1.723 | 0.085 |
| | ESYTC | 2.200 | 1.881 | 2.574 | 9.849 | 0.000 |
| | HEALTH2000 | 2.200 | 1.601 | 3.022 | 4.865 | 0.000 |
| | LR-AUS | 2.180 | 1.580 | 3.007 | 4.747 | 0.000 |
| | SSLS | 2.142 | 1.718 | 2.670 | 6.774 | 0.000 |
| | MACS2 | 2.097 | 1.315 | 3.343 | 3.111 | 0.002 |
| | GP | 2.030 | 1.136 | 3.627 | 2.391 | 0.017 |
| | Z-PROSO | 1.877 | 1.538 | 2.290 | 6.206 | 0.000 |
| | ATP | 1.700 | 1.056 | 2.736 | 2.185 | 0.029 |
| | PYS | 1.607 | 1.017 | 2.538 | 2.034 | 0.042 |
| | ENDPS | 1.338 | 0.988 | 1.812 | 1.883 | 0.060 |
| | ENLSB | 1.303 | 0.636 | 2.668 | 0.724 | 0.469 |
| | MACS1 | 1.290 | 0.758 | 2.194 | 0.939 | 0.348 |
| | IYDS | 1.278 | 0.627 | 2.604 | 0.675 | 0.499 |
| | DLRS | 1.240 | 1.028 | 1.496 | 2.243 | 0.025 |
| | JLS | 1.219 | 0.970 | 1.532 | 1.696 | 0.090 |
| | MUQSP | 1.210 | 0.632 | 2.317 | 0.575 | 0.565 |
| | CHDS | 1.200 | 0.627 | 2.298 | 0.550 | 0.582 |
| Fixed | | 1.736 | 1.616 | 1.864 | 15.162 | 0.000 |
| Random | | 1.707 | 1.487 | 1.960 | 7.596 | 0.000 |

Odds ratio and 95%CI — 0.01 0.1 1 10 100 — Favors Nondepression   Favors Depression

*Note:* AMHC = Adolescent Mental Health Cohort; DLRS = Danish Longitudinal Retrospective Study; GP = Gatehouse Project; HEALTH2000 = Health 2000 Project; LR-AUS = Longitudinal Retrospective Study of American University Students; MUQSP = Mater-University of Queensland Study of Pregnancy and Outcomes; SSLS = Seven Schools Longitudinal Study; Z-PROSO = z-proso Longitudinal Study; see also abbreviations in Figure 7.1.

twice as likely as noninvolved children to be depressed later in life.

The results presented here are based on a report for the Swedish National Council for Crime Prevention in which analyses relevant to the above two meta-analytic reviews were updated, with more recent studies included in the meta-analyses.[11]

Children involved in school bullying (either as bullies or victims) are high-risk youth. The results of the two meta-analyses suggest that high-quality effective antibullying programs should be encouraged. They could be viewed as an early form of public health promotion as well as an early form of crime prevention. These programs can potentially have long-term effects by reducing the future psychosocial maladjustment of the troubled individual (and reducing the associated health, welfare, education, and other costs). In light of evidence on the monetary value of saving a high-risk youth, an effective program for school bullies and victims would have a high benefit-to-cost ratio.[12] The question, therefore, is: How effective are antibullying programs? This is examined next.

## Current research on bullying prevention

It is encouraging that a substantial body of research has already been completed in the area of bullying prevention. A thorough systematic review and meta-analysis on the effectiveness of bullying prevention programs was completed under the aegis of the Campbell Collaboration.[13] A total of 622 reports concerned with bullying prevention were found, and 89 of these reports (describing 53 program evaluations) were included in the review. Stringent methodological quality criteria were set for inclusion or exclusion of evaluations (for example, there had to be comparison of an experimental and control group), so that reductions in the levels of bullying or victimization could safely be attributed to the intervention and not to extraneous factors.

Of the 53 program evaluations, 44 provided data that permitted the calculation of an effect size for bullying or victimization. The meta-analysis of these 44 evaluations showed that overall, school-based antibullying programs are effective. On average, bullying decreased by 20 to 23 percent and victimization by 17 to 20 percent. Program elements and intervention components that were associated with a decrease in bullying and victimization were identified, based on feedback from researchers about the coding of 40 out of 44 programs. The most important components were parent meetings, improved playground supervision, firm disciplinary methods, classroom management, teacher training, and cooperative group work. Programs that were more intensive and had a longer duration were also more effective.

## Risk and protective factors for school bullying and its negative effects

Current research has confirmed that school bullying (perpetration and victimization) uniquely contributes to internalizing and externalizing problems after taking into account preexisting adjustment problems and other major childhood risk factors.[14] However, not all children involved in school bullying go on to experience adjustment difficulties. Some resilient children function better than would be expected and do not follow a criminal career path later in life.[15] These findings are consistent with previous research on protective factors providing resiliency for children from multiproblem milieus.[16]

Various questions subsequently arise. First, what protective factors interrupt the continuity from school bullying to later adverse outcomes? What are the intervening mechanisms that nullify the effect of school bullying on a given outcome? Second, what factors give resiliency to children from multiproblem milieus, enabling them to avoid being involved in school bullying as either perpetrators or victims? In other words, what protective factors buffer the effects of risk factors for bullying perpetration and victimization? These questions can be more adequately addressed using data from prospective longitudinal studies and also by focusing on both risk and protective factors.

Risk-focused prevention has become very popular, based on the idea that offending and other externalizing problems can be reduced by targeting and alleviating risk factors.[17] Following the traditional risk factors approach, an interventionist could investigate risk factors that are related to both childhood bullying and adult offending. It would be expected that the removal of relevant risk factors should reduce the probability of offending (or other adverse outcomes) later in life. To give an example, a recent systematic review and meta-analysis on risk factors predicting children's involvement in school bullying found that the typical school bully is one who exhibits significant externalizing behavior, has both social competence and academic challenges, possesses negative attitudes and beliefs about others, has negative self-related cognitions, has trouble resolving problems with others, and comes from a family environment characterized by conflict and poor parental monitoring.[18] Notably, many of these risk factors are also related to juvenile delinquency and offending.[19] Subsequently, following the traditional risk factors approach, interventionists and practitioners would argue that removal of these risk factors could reduce both bullying and offending and enable children to live well-adjusted lives in the long run.

Although this approach is scientifically sound, it has more recently become clear that prevention and intervention initiatives should expand this traditional approach in such a way that protective factors are also taken into account.[20] Various practical and methodological reasons have been put forward to explain why the traditional risk factors approach would benefit from incorporating the notion of protective factors in the existing analytical framework.

At a practical level, removal of major risk factors from children's lives is often impossible. To give an example, although a recent systematic, meta-analytic review has established the link between parental incarceration and offspring maladjustment, using alternatives to imprisonment is in many cases not acceptable, at least not within the current justice system.[21] At the methodological level, the assumption of cumulative risk effects in predicting cumulative adverse outcomes or increased severity of a specific outcome (multiplicative effects, where the combination of two risk factors has a greater effect than expected on the basis of simple addition) is not always valid.[22]

In order to examine whether a risk factor is a predictor or possible cause for a given outcome, the risk factor needs to be measured before the outcome.[23] Therefore, prospective longitudinal surveys are needed to investigate risk factors and especially whether causal effects can be identified.[24] Future research on school bullying should examine risk and protective factors related to school bullying based on longitudinal studies. Longitudinal research is needed on careers of bullying and victimization: when they begin, how long they persist, and when they end.[25] In addition, variables that influence onset, persistence, and desistance within this longitudinal framework should be studied. The vast majority of current research is based on cross-sectional data, which do not allow examination of whether any given individual, family, or social factor is a correlate, a predictor, or a possible cause of bullying. This problem has important implications for new antibullying initiatives. Program planners need to target causes of bullying behavior and not merely risk markers that are symptoms of this type of problem behavior.

---

## Protective factors in new antibullying initiatives: Some examples

Significant research attention has been directed toward identifying risk factors for bullying and victimization, so that we can now sketch a fairly accurate profile of the characteristics of childhood perpetrators and victims of school bullying.[26] However, this picture is incomplete, and it is time that researchers started investigating what protective factors may moderate the relations between risk factors and the likelihood of children becoming victims and bullies.[27] Researchers should also examine protective factors that interrupt the continuity from bullying (perpetration or victimization) to later adverse outcomes based on longitudinal studies. Some examples of current research on the topic are described below. Guidelines for future research, based on findings from similar research fields, are also presented.

In a short-term longitudinal study, Smith and colleagues found that "escaped victims" (those who were no longer victims after a period of two years) did not differ substantially in terms of their profiles from nonvictims, and they reported a number of successful strategies for dealing with the experience of being bullied, such as talking to someone about incidents or making efforts to find new friends.[28] These victims were less likely than continuing victims to blame themselves for being bullied. A high-quality friendship has been identified as a protective factor that significantly moderates the relationship between bullying behavior and externalizing problems, and further research on the matter is warranted.[29]

Bijttebbier and Vertommen found that victims of school bullying were more likely to use internalizing coping strategies, such as avoiding facing the problem or remaining passive, in dealing with peer relationships.[30] School bullies were more likely to use externalizing coping strategies such as aggression and blaming others. It is possible that good reasoning and problem-solving skills may be a protective factor against school bullying, although no research has examined this topic so far. Findings in similar areas of research are nevertheless suggestive. Werner and Smith, for example, found that good reading, reasoning, and problem-solving skills at age ten were important protective factors among high-risk children who did not develop serious behavioral problems by age eighteen.[31] A high IQ, which is related to good reasoning and problem-solving skills, has also been identified as a protective risk factor. In the E-Risk Study, Jaffee and colleagues concluded that maltreated children who did not become antisocial tended to have high intelligence and to live in low-crime neighborhoods with high social cohesion and informal social control.[32]

Future research on school bullying also needs to examine the extent to which bonding to significant others (such as parents and teachers) is a protective factor against school bullying. Findings in similar areas of research are suggestive. Based on data from the Rochester Youth Development Study, Smith and colleagues found that high-risk children who were resilient (that is, nondelinquent) tended to have good parental supervision and good attachment to parents.[33] Herrenkohl and colleagues, in a longitudinal survey of Pennsylvania children, found that a strong commitment to school, and having parents and peers who disapproved of antisocial behavior, predicted low rates of violence and delinquency among adolescents who had been physically abused as children.[34] Within the area of school bullying, research has found that families protect against the negative effects of bullying victimization.[35]

The protective effects of bonding to teachers against school bullying and its negative effects has, to the best of our knowledge, not been investigated so far.

## Conclusion

Focusing on protective factors and on building resilience of children at risk is a more positive approach, and more attractive to communities, than reducing risk factors, which emphasizes deficits and problems.[36] Within other fields, such as criminology, the evidence regarding protective factors and resilience is at a very initial stage compared with research on risk factors.[37] Protective factors, however, have started to receive increased attention and are considered a key challenge for the next generation of risk assessment research.[38] Research findings on protective factors are even more scattered within the area of school bullying. In the future, bullying agencies need to adopt a risk-and-protection-focused prevention approach as their framework to guide new antibullying initiatives.

It is necessary to develop an assessment instrument that can provide data on empirically identified risk and protective factors for school bullying based on findings from prospective longitudinal research and following guidelines from relevant research in other fields.[39] Possible differences in measurement reliability and validity across gender, age, and racial/ethnic groups of such an instrument should also be examined. Such an instrument would have important applications in prevention need assessment and strategic prevention planning.

The time is ripe to mount a new program of international collaborative research on risk and protective factors against school bullying and its long-term consequences based on prospective longitudinal studies from across the world. Future findings in this area of research will help in the construction and refinement of theories of school bullying, which is currently another neglected area of research.[40]

## Notes

1. Glew, G., Rivara, F., & Feudtner, C. (2000). Bullying: Children hurting children. *Pediatrics in Review*, *21*, 183–190.

2. Ttofi, M. M., & Farrington, D. P. (2008). Bullying: Short-term and long-term effects and the importance of defiance theory in explanation and prevention. *Victims and Offenders*, *3*, 289–312; Farrington, D. P., & Ttofi, M. M. (2009). School-based programs to reduce bullying and victimization. *Campbell Systematic Reviews*, *2009*, 6; Ttofi, M. M., & Farrington, D. P. (2011). Effectiveness of school-based programs to reduce bullying: A systematic and meta-analytic review. *Journal of Experimental Criminology*, *7*, 27–56.

3. From the U.K.: Bullied girl, 15, dies after leaping from bridge onto busy road. (2009). *Daily Mail*, September 18, 2009, http://article.wn.com /view/2009/09/18/Bullied_girl_15_dies_after_leaping_from_bridge_onto _busy_roa/6.

From Wales: School abuse inquiry condemned by commissioner. (2010, April 1). *BBC*. Retrieved from http://news.bbc.co.uk/1/hi/wales/8598136. stm7.

From the United States: Cullen, K. (2010, December 8). Admission of failure. *Boston Globe*. Retrieved from http://www.boston.com/news/local /massachusetts/articles/2010/12/14/admission_of_failure/?s_campaign =8315.

4. Liang, H., Flisher, A. J., & Lombard, C. J. (2007). Bullying, violence, and risk behavior in South African school students. *Child Abuse and Neglect*, *31*(2), 161–171; Smith, P. K., Morita, Y., Junger-Tas, J., Olweus, D., Catalano, R., & Slee, P. (1999). *The nature of school bullying: A cross-national perspective*. London: Routledge.

5. Olweus, D. (1993). *Bullying at school: What we know and what we can do*. Oxford: Blackwell.

6. Olweus, D. (2011). Bullying at school and later criminality: Findings from three Swedish community samples of males. *Criminal Behavior and Mental Health*, *21*, 151–156.

7. Farrington, D. P. (1993). Understanding and preventing bullying. In M. Tonry (Ed.), *Crime and justice* (pp. 381–458). Chicago, IL: University of Chicago Press.

8. Farrington, D. P., Ttofi, M. M., & Lösel, F. (2011). Editorial: School bullying and later offending. *Criminal Behaviour and Mental Health, 21*, 77–79; Ttofi, M. M., Farrington, D. P., & Lösel, F. (2011a). Editorial: Health consequences of school bullying. *Journal of Aggression, Conflict and Peace Research, 3*(2), 60–62.

9. Ttofi, M. M., Farrington, D. P., Lösel, F., & Loeber, R. (2011b). The predictive efficiency of school bullying versus later offending: A systematic/meta-analytic review of longitudinal studies. *Criminal Behaviour and Mental Health, 21*, 80–89.

10. Ttofi, M. M., Farrington, D. P., Lösel, F., & Loeber, R. (2011c). Do the victims of school bullying tend to become depressed later in life? A systematic review and meta-analysis of longitudinal studies. *Journal of Aggression, Conflict and Peace Research, 3*(2), 63–73.

11. Farrington, D. P., Losel, F., Ttofi, M.M., & Theodorakis, N. (2012). *School bullying, depression and offending behaviour later in life: An updated systematic review of longitudinal studies.* Stockholm: Swedish National Council for Crime Prevention.

12. Cohen, M. A., & Piquero, A. R. (2009). New evidence on the monetary value of saving a high risk youth. *Journal of Quantitative Criminology, 25*, 25–49.

13. Farrington & Ttofi. (2009); Ttofi & Farrington. (2011).

14. Ttofi et al. (2011b, 2011c); Farrington et al. (2012).

15. Baldry, A. C., & Farrington, D. P. (2005). Protective factors as moderators of risk factors in adolescence bullying. *Social Psychology of Education, 8*, 263–284; Bowes, L., Maughan, B., Caspi, A., Moffitt, T. E., & Arsenault, L. (2010). Families promote emotional and behavioural resilience to bullying: Evidence of an environmental effect. *Child Psychology and Psychiatry, 51*(7), 809–817; Ttofi, M. M. (2011, April 7). *What factors protect adolescent bullies from developing into criminal offenders?* Adolescence: Exploration and self-regulation of the unknown, Jacobs Foundation Conference, Marbach Castle.

16. Bender, D., & Lösel, F. (1997). Protective and risk effects of peer relations and social support on antisocial behaviour in adolescents from multiproblem milieus. *Journal of Adolescence, 20*, 661–678; Farrington, D. P., & Ttofi, M. M. (2011). Protective and promotive factors in the development of offending. In T. Bliesener, A. Beelman, & M. Stemmler (Eds.), *Antisocial behaviour and crime: Contributions of developmental and evaluation research to prevention and intervention* (pp. 71–88). Gottingen, Germany: Hogrefe.

17. Farrington, D. P. (2000). Explaining and preventing crime: The globalization of knowledge: The American Society of Criminology 1999 Presidential Address. *Criminology, 38*, 1–24.

18. Cook, C. R., Williams, K. R., Guerra, N. G., Kim, T. E., & Sadek, S. (2010). Predictors of school bullying and victimization in childhood and adolescence: A meta-analytic investigation. *School Psychology Quarterly, 25*, 65–83.

19. Farrington, D. P. (2012). Childhood risk factors for young adult offending: Onset and persistence. In. F. Losel, A. E. Bottoms, & D. P. Farrington (Eds.), *Young adult offenders: Lost in transition?* London: Routledge, in press.

20. Farrington & Ttofi. (2011).

21. Murray, J., Farrington, D. P., Sekol, I., Olsen, R. F. (2009). Effects of parental imprisonment on child antisocial behaviour and mental health: A systematic review. *Campbell Systematic Reviews, 2009, 4.*

22. Loeber, R., Farrington, D. P., Stouthamer-Loeber, M., & Van Kammen, W. B. (1998). *Antisocial behavior and mental health problems: Explanatory factors in childhood and adolescence.* Mahwah, NJ: Erlbaum.

23. Farrington, D. P., Loeber, R., & Ttofi, M. M. (2011). Risk and protective factors for offending. In B. C. Welsh & D. P. Farrington (Eds.), *The Oxford handbook of crime prevention.* New York, NY: Oxford University Press, in press.

24. Murray, J., Farrington, D. P., & Eisner, M. P. (2009). Drawing conclusions about causes from systematic reviews of risk factors: The Cambridge Quality Checklists. *Journal of Experimental Criminology, 5,* 1–23.

25. Farrington. (1993).

26. Cook et al. (2010).

27. Bollmer, J. M., Milich, R., Harris, M. J., & Maras, M. A. (2005). A friend in need: The role of friendship quality as a protective factor in peer victimization and bullying. *Journal of Interpersonal Violence, 20*(6), 701–712.

28. Smith, P. K., Talamelli, L., Coiwe, H., Naylor, P., & Chauhan, P. (2004). Profiles of non-victims, escaped victims, continuing victims and new victims of school bullying. *British Journal of Educational Psychology, 74,* 565–581.

29. Bollmer et al. (2005).

30. Bijttebbier, P., & Vertommen, H. (1998). Coping with peer argument in school-aged children with bully/victim problems. *British Journal of Educational Psychology, 68,* 387–394.

31. Werner, E. E., & Smith, R. S. (1992). *Overcoming the odds: Children from birth to adulthood.* Ithaca, NY: Cornell University Press.

32. Jaffee, S. R., Caspi, A., Moffitt, T. E., Polo-Tomas, M., & Taylor, A. (2007). Individual, family, and neighborhood factors distinguish resilient from non-resilient maltreated children: A cumulative stressors model. *Child Abuse and Neglect, 31,* 231–253.

33. Smith, C. A., Lozotte, A. J., Thornberry, T. P., & Krohn, M. D. (1995). Resilient youth: Identifying factors that prevent high-risk youth from engaging in delinquency and drug use. In J. L. Hagan (Ed.), *Delinquency and disrepute in the life course* (pp. 217–247). Greenwich, CT: JAI Press.

34. Herrenkohl, T. I., Tajima, E. A., Witney, S. D., & Huang, B. (2005). Protection against antisocial behavior in children exposed to physically abusive discipline. *Journal of Adolescent Health, 36,* 457–465.

35. Bowes et al. (2010); Cluver, L., Bowes, L., & Gardner, F. (2010). Risk and protective factors for bullying victimization among AIDS-affected and vulnerable children in South Africa. *Child Abuse and Neglect, 34*(10), 793–803.

36. Farrington et al. (2011); Pollard, J. A., Hawkins, J. D., & Arthur, M. W. (1999). Risk and protection: Are both necessary to understand diverse behavioural outcomes in adolescence? *Social Work Research*, *23*, 145–158.

37. Werner, E. E. (2000). Protective factors and individual resilience. In J. P. Shonkoff & S. P. Meisels (Eds.), *Handbook of early childhood prevention* (pp. 115–132). Cambridge: Cambridge University Press.

38. Farrington, D. P. (2007). Advancing knowledge about desistance. *Journal of Contemporary Criminal Justice*, *23*, 125–134.

39. Rennie, C. E., & Dolan, M. C. (2010). The significance of protective factors in the assessment of risk. *Criminal Behavior and Mental Health*, *20*, 8–22.

40. Smith, P. K. (2010). Cyberbullying: The European perspective. In J. Mora-Merchan & T. Jaeger (Eds.), *Cyberbullying: A cross-national comparison* (pp. 7–19). Landau: Verlag Emprische Padagogik.

MARIA M. TTOFI *is the Jacobs Foundation Postdoctoral Research Fellow at the Institute of Criminology, University of Cambridge.*

DAVID P. FARRINGTON *is a professor of psychological criminology at the Institute of Criminology, University of Cambridge.*

# 8

# Resources

## Standards for evidence-based practice

- What Works Clearinghouse: http://ies.ed.gov/ncee/wwc/
- Best Evidence Encyclopedia: www.bestevidence.org
- Campbell Collaboration: www.campbellcollaboration.org
- U.K.-Based Evidence for Policy and Practice Information and Co-Ordinating Centre: www.eppi.ioe.ac.uk

## Bernese Program against Victimization in Kindergarten and Elementary School

- Program home pages: http://www.praevention-alsaker.unibe.ch/, http://www.kanderstegdeclaration.com/

### Further Resources
Alsaker, F. D. (2012). *Mutig gegen Mobbing in Kindergarten und Schule*. Bern: Huber Verlag.
Valkanover, S., Alsaker, F. D., Welten, R., Svrcek, A., & Kauer, M. (2004). *Mobbing ist kein Kinderspiel. Medienpaket zur Prävention in Kindergarten und Schule*. Bern: Schulverlag blmv.

## Zero program

- Program home pages: http://saf.uis.no/programmes/Zero/

### Further Resources
Roland, E., & Vaaland, G. (2006). *ZERO teacher's guide to the Zero Anti-Bullying Programme*. Stavanger: Centre for Behavioural Research, University of Stavanger.

## KiVa antibullying program

- Program home pages: www.kivakoulu.fi (an international Web site, www.kivaprogram.com, is in preparation)

NEW DIRECTIONS FOR YOUTH DEVELOPMENT, NO. 133, SPRING 2012 © WILEY PERIODICALS, INC.
Published online in Wiley Online Library (wileyonlinelibrary.com) • DOI: 10.1002/yd.20010

*Further Resources*

Salmivalli, C., Kärnä, A., & Poskiparta, E. (2010). Development, evaluation, and diffusion of a national anti-bullying program, KiVa. In B. Doll, W. Pfohl, & J. Yoon (Eds.), *Handbook of youth prevention science* (pp. 240–254). New York: Routledge.

Salmivalli, C., Kärnä, A., & Poskiparta, E. (2011). Counteracting bullying in Finland: The KiVa program and its effects on different forms of being bullied. *International Journal for Behavioral Development, 35,* 405–411.

## *fairplayer.manual*

• Program home pages: www.fairplayer.de, www.degede.de
• Film: http://www.youtube.com/watch?v=64Be5hBmL18

*Further Resources*

Scheithauer, H., & Bull, H. D. (2008). *fairplayer.manual: Förderung von sozialen Kompetenzen und Zivilcourage—Prävention von Bullying und Schulgewalt.* Göttingen: Vandenhoeck & Ruprecht.

Schultze-Krumbholz, A., Scheithauer, H., & Braun, D. (2009). *Zum Umgang mit Bullying und Cyberbullying in der Schule: Eine Handreichung für Lehrerinnen und Lehrer im Bundesland Bremen.* Bremen: Unfallkasse Freie Hansestadt Bremen. http://www.unfallkasse.bremen.de/pdf-dl.php?id=18&type=1

## *ViSC Social Competence Program*

• Program home pages: http://www.univie.ac.at/wisk.psychologie/, www.gemeinsam-gegen-gewalt.at

*Further Resources*

Kessler, D. & Strohmeier, D. (2009). *Gewaltprävention an Schulen.* ÖZEPS Reihe. Handreichungen für Lehrer/innen aller Schularten und Studierende. Vienna: Österreichisches Zentrum für Persönlichkeitsbildung und soziales Lernen in Kooperation mit der Uni Wien im Auftrag des.

Spiel, C., & Strohmeier, D. (2011). National strategy for violence prevention in the Austrian public school system: Development and implementation. *International Journal of Behavioral Development, 35,* 412–418.

# Index

Alsaker, F. D., 3, 15, 28, 99
Antibullying programs. *See* Bernese
    program; fairplayer.manual; KiVa
    antibullying program; ViSC Social
    Competence Program; Zero
    program
Antibullying programs, as crime
    prevention, 6, 86–87, 89
Assistants, defined, 56, 64

Bernese program: brief description of,
    3–4; conclusions on, 25; evaluation
    of, 23–25; ideas behind, 16–18;
    resources on, 99; six modules
    in, 18–23; victimization in
    kindergarten and, 15–16
Bijttebbier, P., 93
Bull, H. D., 5, 55, 61, 70, 100
Bully, description of typical school, 91
Bully/Victim Questionnaire (BVQ),
    61, 64
Bullying: adverse outcomes from,
    56, 86–89; defined, 1, 8, 30;
    detecting, 3, 7, 8–9, 19, 76;
    empirical knowledge about, 17–18;
    responding to, 9–10; rules against,
    20–21
*Bullying: Scenes from Children's Lives*, 30
Bullying prevention: current research
    on, 6, 34–36, 89–90; evidence-
    based programs for, 10–11; in
    kindergarten, 15–25; ViSC Social
    Competence Program for, 71–81;
    in Zero program, 31–32. *See also*
    Antibullying programs
Burger, C., 81
Bystanders' behaviors, influencing,
    42–43, 44, 46, 56–57

Classroom leadership, importance of, 31
Computer games, antibullying, 46,
    50–51
Conversations, problem-solving, 32,
    76–77

Crime prevention, antibullying
    programs as, 6, 86–87, 89
Cyberbullying, 36, 55, 67

Depression and bullying victimization,
    16, 43, 56, 87–89

Escaped victims, 93
Evidence-based practice: defined, 10;
    standards for, 11, 99

fairplayer.manual: aims of, 57–58; brief
    description of, 5; conclusions
    on, 64, 66; evaluation of, 60–64;
    further development of, 66–67;
    main message of, 58, 59; relational
    aggression and, 55, 58, 65, 66;
    resources on, 100; teacher training
    for, 59–60; whole-school approach
    for, 59; on youtube.com, 67
Farrington, D. P., 6, 25, 85, 98
Finnish school system, 41–42, 51.
    *See also* KiVa antibullying program
Friendship, as protective factor, 93

German schools, bullying in, 55, 66

Handling Bullying Questionnaire
    (HBQ), 81
Herrenkohl, T. I., 94
Hess, M., 5, 55, 69
Hoffmann, C., 5, 71, 84
Homosexual students and bullying, 36

Idsøe, T., 31
Ireland, modified Zero program in, 34

Jaffee, S. R., 93

Kandersteg Declaration against
    Bullying, 20
Kessler, D., 100
Kindergarten, victimization in, 15–16.
    *See also* Bernese program

KiVa antibullying program: description of, 4–5; development of, 41–42; evaluation of, 48–51; goals of, 42–43; implementation of, 44–48; resources on, 99–100

Limits, teaching children how to set, 22–23

Manifesto Against Bullying, Norwegian, 30, 34, 36
Midthassel, U. V., 4, 29, 39

Nicolaides, S., 9
Noam, G. G., 1, 2, 3, 7, 13
Norwegian Manifesto Against Bullying, 30, 34, 36

Olweus, D., 11, 29, 30, 66, 86

Parents: good attachment to, 93–94; information for, 46–47; involving, 25, 32, 33
Participant Role Questionnaire (PRQ), 64
Poskiparta, E., 4, 41, 53
Protective factors in antibullying initiatives, 92–94

Questionnaire, Bully/Victim (BVQ), 61, 64
Questionnaire, Handling Bullying (HBQ), 81
Questionnaire, Participant Role (PRQ), 64

Reinforcers, defined, 43, 56, 64
Relational aggression, 55, 58, 65, 66
Research on bullying prevention, 6, 34–36, 89–90
Resiliency in children, 90, 94
Resources, additional, 99–100
Roland, E., 4, 11, 29, 30, 31, 39, 76, 77, 99
Rule of silence, 19–20
Rules against bullying, 20–21
Ryan, W., 66

Salmivalli, C., 4, 41, 53, 100
Scheithauer, H., 5, 55, 61, 69, 100
Schiller, E.-M., 5, 71, 84
School Environment Survey, 34

Schultze-Krumbholz, A., 5, 55, 70, 100
Sexual orientation and bullying, 36
Silence, rule of, 19–20
Smith, C. A., 94
Smith, J. D., 66
Smith, P. K., 9, 93
Smith, R. S., 93
Social competence, developing, 22–23
Social Competence Program. See ViSC Social Competence Program
Spiel, C., 5, 71, 84, 100
Spröber, N., 66
Stefanek, E., 5, 71, 84
Strohmeier, D., 1, 2, 3, 5, 7, 13, 71, 84, 100

Tattling on peers, 21–22
Teachers: Bernese program modules for, 3–4, 18–23; consistent behavior of, 21; detection of bullying by, 8–9, 19; fairplayer.manual training for, 59–60; insecurity of, 17, 21; problem-solving conversations and, 32, 76–77; role of, 16–17, 21, 22; ViSC program training for, 75–78
Toda, Y., 9
Together Against Violence (Austria's national strategy), 5, 72
Ttofi, M. M., 6, 25, 85, 98

Vaaland, G., 76, 77, 99
Valkanover, S., 3, 15, 28, 99
Vertommen, H., 93
ViSC Social Competence Program: brief description of, 5–6; class project, 78–80; coaches in, 73–75; goals and target groups of, 72–73; implementation of, 75; large-scale evaluation of, 80–81; resources on, 100; teacher training in, 75–78

Werner, E. E., 93

Yanagida, T., 81

Zero program: content, 30–33; description of, 4, 29; development of, 29–30; implementation strategy, 33–34; in Ireland, 34; ongoing efforts and, 26–37; research on, 34–36; resources on, 99

NEW DIRECTIONS FOR YOUTH DEVELOPMENT

# ORDER FORM SUBSCRIPTION AND SINGLE ISSUES

## DISCOUNTED BACK ISSUES:

Use this form to receive 20% off all back issues of *New Directions for Youth Development*.
All single issues priced at **$23.20** (normally $29.00)

TITLE                                          ISSUE NO.          ISBN

_____     _____     _____
_____     _____     _____
_____     _____     _____

*Call 888-378-2537 or see mailing instructions below. When calling, mention the promotional code JBNND
to receive your discount. For a complete list of issues, please visit www.josseybass.com/go/ndyd*

## SUBSCRIPTIONS: (1 YEAR, 4 ISSUES)

☐ New Order          ☐ Renewal

| | | |
|---|---|---|
| U.S. | ☐ Individual: $89 | ☐ Institutional: $281 |
| CANADA/MEXICO | ☐ Individual: $89 | ☐ Institutional: $321 |
| ALL OTHERS | ☐ Individual: $113 | ☐ Institutional: $355 |

*Call 888-378-2537 or see mailing and pricing instructions below.
Online subscriptions are available at www.onlinelibrary.wiley.com*

## ORDER TOTALS:

Issue / Subscription Amount: $ _____

Shipping Amount: $ _____
*(for single issues only – subscription prices include shipping)*

**Total Amount:** $ _____

SHIPPING CHARGES:

First Item          $6.00
Each Add'l Item     $2.00

*(No sales tax for U.S. subscriptions. Canadian residents, add GST for subscription orders. Individual rate subscriptions must
be paid by personal check or credit card. Individual rate subscriptions may not be resold as library copies.)*

## BILLING & SHIPPING INFORMATION:

☐ **PAYMENT ENCLOSED:** *(U.S. check or money order only. All payments must be in U.S. dollars.)*

☐ **CREDIT CARD:**  ☐ VISA  ☐ MC  ☐ AMEX

Card number _____ Exp. Date _____

Card Holder Name_____ Card Issue # _____

Signature _____ Day Phone _____

☐ **BILL ME:** *(U.S. institutional orders only. Purchase order required.)*

Purchase order # _____
Federal Tax ID 13559302 • GST 89102-8052

Name _____

Address_____

Phone_____ E-mail_____

Copy or detach page and send to:     **John Wiley & Sons, One Montgomery Street, Suite 1200,
San Francisco, CA 94104-4594**

Order Form can also be faxed to:     **888-481-2665**          PROMO JBNND